CONCILIUM

Religion in the Seventies

CONCILIUM

New Series: Volume 10, Number 9: Moral Theology

POWER AND THE WORD OF GOD

Edited by
Franz Bockle
Jacques-Marie Pohier

Herder and Herder

1973
HERDER AND HERDER NEW YORK
815 Second Avenue
New York 10017

ISBN: 0–8164–2574–4

Cum approbatione Ecclesiastica

Library of Congress Catalog Card Number: 73–6431

Printed in the United States

CONTENTS

PART II
BULLETIN

PART III
DOCUMENTATION CONCILIUM

PART I
ARTICLES

Georges Lavau

The Power Game

IN THE last two decades the only sociology of power—in the West at least—to have been accorded a scientific status is a sociology of "appeasement" which maintains that there is no such thing as a conspiracy of powers. They are said to be multiple, split-up and, in their specialized spheres, to superimpose on one another only incompletely and exceptionally. Under normal conditions there is relative equilibrium between them. Therefore nothing should occur to disturb these "normal" conditions.

This sociology of appeasement is designed primarily as a response to a "popular" opinion: that which suspects the existence of some hidden power, an "invisible hand" ruling all the major sectors of human activity and pulling all the strings in order to satisfy the interests of a closed and homogeneous group. It answers above all a rival sociology which affirms that there is a "power élite" whose form of domination is not specialized but general, and that direct or indirect control of all really significant powers of various kinds assures the hegemony of this élite. Despite legal ploys and constitutional masks this hegemony is tantamount to absolute power.

There is hardly any need to stress the fact that I have omitted any demonstration of these theses and considerably simplified the positions held. However schematic it may be, this account nevertheless leads the reader to inquire into the following proposition: What if the two sociologies in question posed the problem badly and left others in obscurity?

The fact that in every society there are various sources of power

9

and multiple groups between which conflicts are generally latent or open; that, consequently, it is unusual to find a single absolute power in all areas in the hands of one homogeneous group, with an acute awareness of its class interests and with the unyielding intention of satisfying its own interests alone, is inadequate evidence. That in almost all societies there may be areas of freedom and delimited spheres of power or means of resistance and pressure for almost all (even poorly organized) groups is probable (though not always proven).

But that is not saying much. At the risk of appearing scientific, I would say that my interest is only awakened at the empirical verification and exact measurement of phenomena: what quanta of power, freedom and guarantees are there on this side and on that? In what areas, at what cost, does one or the other obtain amounts (comparable or not) of power? Who has a lot and who has less? Who generally appears in this type of coalition, and who features in that type? How, finally, by peaceful or violent processes, at the cost of heavy or light sacrifices, does this distribution of powers change? Without such verifications, talk of "equilibrium" is useless. Yet the very least of these processes of verification comes up against very tough technical and theoretical problems.

But of course there are other difficulties.

All theories of the balance of power depend on the (generally implicit) presupposition that power is a constant quantity within a given social whole. Any degree of power possessed by a group is therefore that degree that the others do not possess. Any degree of power taken or acquired by a group is that degree removed from those who possessed all power. This is the so-called sum-zero power hypothesis. The multiplicity of powers (even if these different powers are unequal) and the changes in the distribution of these powers therefore go to prove that there is no *one* power élite. But this hypothesis is contestable, as we shall see.

On the other hand, man (of all species) features that peculiarity of desiring and possessing the capacity to modify and remodel his social organizations; to create new, variously structured groups; to create new social relations; and to change cultural models and institutionalized value systems.[1] This social innova-

[1] Cf. J. W. Lapierre, *Essai sur le fondement du pouvoir politique* (1968).

tion is not without struggles between those who want to preserve and those who want to change; between different groups who stand for different plans for social reorganization. But one of the most intriguing problems raised by the sociology of power is the inequality of conditions of struggle and defence. For some groups, struggle and defence are or could be simultaneously possible, permissible and even encouraged. In the most favourable cases it is the State itself which assures them with all the support of its dignity and reputation for service in the general interest. Or they may be encouraged by accordance with the most official cultural schemata, or by the occupation of influential and dominative social or economic positions. For other groups, however, struggle and defence are incomparably more difficult and should be rewarded with a much higher cost. Most of the time they have first to surmount a number of obstacles—legal, political, cultural and economic. The old quarrel—are there dominant and dominated classes?—is only fully meaningful if posed in regard to the struggle for or against social innovation.

In all (even slightly) complex societies, multiple groups are structured around interests and values. Occasionally some of these interests and values are complementary and associated; occasionally they conflict.

Sometimes, too, several of these groups go after objectives which are so non-competitive that they hardly run the risk of rivalry, except to the degree that their requests for help and subsidies force the donating authorities to arbitrate between them. Each of them has power (over its members and over things) and powers. Even though there are (rarely permanent) coalitions between them, they do not merge. The political power with authority over them usually acknowledges their special spheres of liberty and independence. It ensures for at least some of them a right of representation within defined limits. Sometimes it even goes so far as to concede to some of them means of obstructing its will or of taking part in the development and execution of its decisions.

Of course guarantees, rights, concessions and participation in certain acts of power are not accorded to all with equal generosity, and the least favoured often receive powers only when necessity, fear or utility forces the issue. One thing in any case can be admitted as hypothetical: it is neither part of the functional logic or political power, nor in the interest of those who exercise it, to allow the rise or crystallization of an imbalance so to the profit of privileged groups that it could give rise to revolts and coalitions among the excluded. For the same reasons, the holders of political power usually strive not to seem organically confused with a definite group.

For Arthur Bentley and some of his present-day disciples, for example,[2] the operation of the political system is only the result of an opposition of groups with differing interests which, directly or indirectly, translate or cause to be translated into political actions the sum of their compromises and their victories; the State itself being, on this market, only one "interest group" among others, a little more proficiently equipped (if it relies on popular suffrage) because it represents latent, widely diffused interests which are not undertaken by specialized groups.

More highly-nuanced and dependent on empirical verification (though limited to local power in an average U.S. town), the polyarchy theory of Robert Dahl is not basically different.[3] For Dahl political power depends on bargaining, not between groups but between rival leaders who are very specialized in their functions and domains. The most influential among them never have any undivided power, and they take part in an unending struggle where not everything is permitted, since it takes place under the supervision of electors and parties anxious to maximize their gains and to minimize their losses. The inequalities in the means of influence (political, economic, administrative, social or cultural) are not cumulative, and there is a dispersion of the political resources controlled by the leaders. Even if Dahl is careful to emphasize that the polyarchic model works only if at least two conditions are simultaneously satisfied (that there should be a broad preponderance in the social whole of a solid consensus on the goals and means of social action; and that at the same time there should be a minimum equalization of socio-economic conditions and an unceasing renewal of élites), these conditions do not alter the general conclusion: there is a multiplicity of sources

[2] A. Bentley, *The Process of Government* (1908); David Truman, *The Governmental Process* (1951).
[3] Robert Dahl, *Who Governs?* (1951).

of power; these can emanate from political or administrative positions, but also from socio-economic positions, as from the control of means of information or specialized techniques.

By various analyses, David Riesman arrived at quite proximate conclusions[4] when he described North-American society as split into a large number of "veto groups" directed more towards defence than towards rule, but capable at certain moments and for certain problems, of a circumstantial authority. According to Riesman, the only two stable elements of a "dominant class" in the U.S.A. are the bureaucracy and the governmental authorities (both being heterogeneous), but these two fractions are obliged to take into account veto groups which, in particular situations, force the public authorities to consider their interests. Ralf Dahrendorf of course objected against Riesman that this analysis did not try to discover if some of these groups benefited, in a quasi-permanent manner, from a privileged position vis-à-vis the party in power and, more generally, vis-à-vis the majority of public authorities with the most effective public powers.[5]

Of course it is possible to add a number of specifications and correctives to the theses just adumbrated,[6] but hardly anyone contests their general import. Dahrendorf, while admitting that class conflicts have not disappeared from so-called post-capitalist societies, also states: "... political conflict is always a circumstantial conflict between individuals who are momentarily in power and those who are excluded from power.... The individuals in power and those without power are, in principle at least, interchangeable." He adds that, if no change occurs for long periods and if the same party remains in power without modifying its politics, conflicts will normally remain localized and attenuated since most interests and veto groups will be alternatively recognized and satisfied.

A number of Marxist theoreticians—within certain limits and in a quite different context—acknowledge the non-unitary nature of power. For instance Antonio Gramsci:[7] "The dominant group

[4] *The Lonely Crowd* (1948).
[5] Ralf Dahrendorf, *Classes and Class Conflicts in Industrial Society* (1970).
[6] See especially Pierre Birnbaum, *La structure du pouvoir aux Etats-Unis* (1970).
[7] *Note sul Machiavelli, sulla politica e sullo Stato moderno.*

[in a hegemonic system] is co-ordinated in actuality with the general interests of subordinate groups, and the life of the State is conceived as a continual formation and a continual overcoming of unstable balances... between the interests of the basic group and those of subordinate groups: balances in which the interests of the dominant group triumph except in the area of the meanest economico-corporative interest." Gramsci acknowledges that intellectuals attached to the basic class and characterized as "functionaries of the superstructure" have to "separate themselves from [that] class in order to unite with it more closely, in order to be an authentic superstructure and not merely an inorganic and indistinct element of the economic structure." Nicos Poulantzas, studying the implications of comes of Marx's analyses of the internal divisions of the French bourgeoisie of 1848, discerns the "deep splitting... of the bourgeois class into class-antagonistic fractions": "Left to themselves, classes and fractions at the level of political domination not only exhaust themselves in internal friction but, more often, founder in contradictions which make them incapable of politic government."[8]

For that reason, and in order to repress that situation, the State exists, for it alone is able (because it retains a relative autonomy in regard to these rival fractions) to offer unity to what Poulantzas significantly calls the "power bloc".

I do not want to suggest that there is neither agreement nor even continuity between Bentley–Dahl and Gramsci–Poulantzas: for the former there are distinct and shared powers and no unique power élite; for the latter the multiplicity of powers does not prevent the existence of a power bloc and the hegemony of one class or an "historic bloc". I want only to suggest that the hypothesis of the "multiplicity" of power and powers (which I think is partly verifiable within certain limits) cannot by itself offer any certain and categorical conclusion.

The "sum-zero power" hypothesis is as "true" as, for example, that of competition pure and simple: it is a theoretical model with an heuristic function, but not a summary of actuality. That is not to say, it does not correspond to *part* of the actuality. It is often true that the powers acquired by a group have been taken

[8] *Pouvoir politique et classes sociales* (1968), p. 324.

at the expense of another group; and even if these powers have not been acquired from others, but, for example, by reason of a novel increase of productive forces unexploited until then, these extended powers increase the relative power of the innovating group and limit correlatively that of other groups. But a whole range of diverse situations can arise.

A dominant group can more or less spontaneously surrender powers and prerogatives which have become superfluous, troublesome or dangerous. It will be all the more prepared to do without them and even to redistribute them to other groups or fractions of groups if it loses nothing in the process, even though it may not gain anything. And this can happen quite often. By the "opening" offered to a few groups the limits of the coalition are extended, beneficiary groups are dissociated, the enemies' frontline is breached, and a less partisan image is created. It may be necessary to pay for these advantages with a few concessions but they are calculated meticulously and care is taken to ensure that the beneficiaries can make only a rigorously controlled use of their gain. A dominant class or an administrative group can surrender more or less coercive powers if it discovers that these means can be advantageously replaced by more economic and subtle means, the effectiveness of which may be less direct but more lasting: cultural conditioning, psychological manipulation and incitement to "compromise" with the system. When cultural and social integration progresses, there are increasingly less disadvantages in the shape of reasons for power—or certain aspects of power—to be shared with people who have accepted principles and rules and who, even in a purely passive way, have become its supports. Moreover, it is the best means of ensuring at least cost the defence of the very basic interests of the dominant categories against those who still reject social, political and cultural integration in whole or part, and consequently find themselves isolated. If the "sum-zero power" hypothesis comes anywhere near concrete reality it is only within the circle of the "integrated" (I hesitate to say "the privileged").

Surely there is no need to remark that this hypothesis postulates that the various powers are very comparable in value and can be divided into lots of equal value. Ultimately this means the admission of a quasi-equivalence between influence and power—

an equivalence which is not far from being posed by sociologists such as Talcott Parsons and Robert Dahl. Here again inconclusive theoretical disputes are of much less interest than rigorously controlled empirical verifications. The latter are rare, but those that exist do not in any way confirm such postulates.

At least as a counter-hypothesis (one more fruitful than that of "sum-zero power"), it is possible to suggest that, under certain conditions, there may be a "concert" or "sharing" of powers, a differentiated distribution of powers, a political, economic and social democracy without any very significant effect (even if it is "better" than something else—an *important* problem, but *another* problem) on the *general* domination of a group or bloc.

It is appropriate to define "domination" in the present context. The reasons for which groups oppose and rival one another in a society are innumerable (the less profound, though not always the less consequential, reasons may have to do with wholly personal motives of their leaders). Nevertheless it is possible to agree that among these reasons the most serious derive from the fact that the existing social order, established social relations and values, are or can be more or less profoundly overthrown, and may in any case give rise to the creation of new organizations, to expensive ventures and brutal and long-drawn-out struggles. These may be patriotic struggles to build a nation and obtain liberation from external domination. They may be struggles of the bourgeoisie to alter and extend—or build—the bases of its power. They may be struggles to change a value system. Or struggles to integrate with a larger community or to reunite separated "brethren". Or class struggles to change the relations of production. . . . There is a gamut of possibilities.

But a given society at a particular moment always depends on a certain relation of forces, on a social structure, and on a certain "equilibrium" between groups; it selects and causes to be taught certain values while it tolerates others as residual or alternative values, but condemns some more or less rigorously. Some groups are (or come to be) satisfied with this state of affairs, whereas others want to make it more or less in agreement with, or better adjusted to, their already largely satisfied interests; yet others are indifferent or not in a position to imagine or desire any change; and, finally some—and not always necessarily the most deprived in a particular area (position in the production process, cultural or technical horizons, political advantages, ecological dispersion) —find it intolerable.

What has to be studied is the inequality of the conditions in which these various groups are placed in relation to one another in their struggle for these goals. Powerful economic forces may offer parties and candidates continually superior financial resources, and may obtain (by publicity or otherwise) very widely distributed information media, together with the services of the best engineers and the most competent individuals; and may "cream off" the best civil servants (whose educational expenses have been paid for by all taxpayers) and offer them the advantages of non-governmental service.

Those educational and university institutions show a "statistical" tendency (sometimes as a result of "social barriers" and of constraints inherent in certain "cultural models") to reproduce in a slightly different form the given social relations and social structure;[9] therefore it is within groups representing these economic forces or within groups which are allied with them (or which aspire to identification with them) that the majority of recruits for managerial and administrative posts are found, together with those intellectuals who will obtain power in their turn; whereas, as Gramsci pointed out, the working class (or the peasant "class") is generally forced to import intellectuals from without. The objective coalition of the groups which are thus in a position of dominance by virtue of social positions and cultural and technical means will also have easier access to facilities offered by the political power and the instruments of the State. The very independence of the State in regard to the bare "injunctions" of groups—of *all* groups—may prove a (more or less easily deflected) irritation to those in power, but it is also a passport and a certificate of innocence, even though not a sufficient advantage (quite the contrary: the rules of the game are most harmful to those in the least favourable positions) for those who have little power. Rarely do more or less innocent mechanisms such as electoral systems and the constituency divisions, non-exemption from processes of law, the right to work, and police surveillance operate against

[9] Here I rely particularly on the work of Alain Girard, Vivianne Isambert-Jamatti, Pierre Bourdieu and Jean-Claude Passeron (all in France).

those in power. The very definition of delinquency does not escape distortion under the pressure of the cultural images which a society of stereotyped modes of behaviour constructs for one social category or another.

Translated by John Griffiths

Jos Jaspars

The Power of the Majority

IN ONE of his surrealistic plays, the Roumano-French writer, Eugène Ionesco, had all the denizens of a small provincial town turning one by one into rhinoceroses.[1] Although Ionesco is seldom given to commenting on his work, the meaning of this full-scale metamorphosis is not hard to guess. The play has never been performed in Russia, for example, because the text does not make it sufficiently clear that rhinoceroses are politically right-wing.[2] At the moment, however, I am not concerned with the ideological import of Ionesco's play but with the psychological process that works itself out in the main character. Even when the first rhinoceros goes tearing past, he is hardly shaken at all. The second rhino does cause some astonishment; but the real drama only begins the next day, when his best friend turns into a rhino before his very eyes. To begin with, he still doesn't take the thing seriously; but when his friend tries to convince him that rhinos are living creatures with as much right to exist as human beings, he is totally bewildered. He turns tail and shuts himself up in his room, while the transformation spreads through the town like an epidemic. He no longer feels sure of himself and begins to wonder whether he really is immune from this sickness. He feels less and less self-confident. Is his friend right? Will norms and values all have to be revised? Will life have to

[1] Eugène Ionesco, *Rhinoceros* (London, 1962).
[2] Thus Ionesco, in an interview with a journalist from the French weekly, *L'Expresse*. In the same interview Ionesco mentions that in fact there were also problems over the production in the United States, because the main character in the play calls on his friend without letting him know in advance by telephone.

be reconstructed on new foundations? Isn't it he himself who is wrong? At the last moment he regains control of himself and makes up his mind to take a stand against the thick-skinned lot who now form an overwhelming majority.

I. The Majority under Laboratory Conditions

The psychological process depicted in dramatic terms by Ionesco in his *Rhinoceros* is one of the most important issues in the field of social psychology. The influence which a majority can exert on the individual has been subject to thorough investigation by social psychologists since 1956. It was in that year that the American psychologist Asch published a series of research studies on "independence" (i.e., self-reliance) and conformism, with the subtitle "A minority of one against a unanimous majority".[3] The scheme of the original piece of research is simple enough. In an observational experiment, a human "guinea pig" is confronted with a majority finding that is obviously false. His task is to indicate which of three linear sections is identical in length with a standard line. It is such an easy task that when those taking part in the experiment are requested to perform it on their own, the incidence of wrong decisions is less than 0·5 per cent. But if the experiment is done in a group and if all the others taking part—acting on the experimenter's instructions, of course—come up with wrong answers, then 30 to 40 per cent of the "uninstructed" subject's findings turn out to be erroneous, when each person has to state his verdict aloud. The process that occurs with the "guinea pig", who does not know that all the other participants are in league with the investigator, closely resembles the inner conflict experienced by the chief character in *Rhinoceros*. The first wrong finding he is still able to refute. But when all the others taking part give, one after another, answers obviously in conflict with his own perception, he becomes uncertain. At first he will look for an explanation in external factors such as a false interpretation on his part of the instructions or the position he has adopted vis-à-vis the lines. But as the experiment proceeds, a strong doubt emerges as to the

[3] S. E. Asch, *Studies in Independence and Conformity. A Minority of One Against a Unanimous Majority* (New York, 1956), 70, No. 416.

rightness of his own judgment and then comes a nagging sus-
picion that the reason must be looked for in hitherto unsuspected
deficiencies which now threaten to show themselves and may
lead to adverse criticism on the part of the group. Some people
are able to overcome such misgivings. In spite of their doubts,
they feel compelled to state what they see. Yet in a much greater
number of instances than one might expect the patently false
conclusion of the majority is accepted.

How is that possible? Why do we in such large measure accept
the verdict of the majority, although knowing it to be wrong?
Is it only certain types of people—conformists—who will accept
the verdict of the group? Do we encounter a similar result when
the decision has to do not with linear sections but with matters
of real importance?

II. THE PRECONDITIONS OF INDEPENDENCE

Asch's experiment raised numerous questions of this sort and
has led to quite a number of experiments centred on the circumstances in which the individual will accommodate himself to
the majority verdict. The conditions investigated separate out
into several groups of factors: the nature of the issue on which a
judgment has to be made, the characteristics of the majority, the
peculiar qualities of the individual, the relation between the individual and the majority and the way in which the individual's
finding is solicited.

1. *The subject-matter*

How important is the subject-matter? Can the group make a
person believe anything and everything in this way?

To discover any regular component in the results achieved by
research the sensible thing is to define the subject-matter in relation to the person concerned. It goes without saying that someone who has a better grip on the subject in question, relatively
to most of the group, will not allow himself to be influenced so
much. However, it would not even appear to be necessary for
the individual to be actually better qualified than the majority.
What does seem to be essential here is the feeling of certitude he
has in the "judgment situation". But this feeling of certainty or

confidence in one's own judgment does not depend exclusively on somebody's personality or past experience: it is also a function of the object of the judgment and the degree of difficulty presented by the task.

2. *The group*

The second factor of importance in accounting for the influence a majority can exert on the judgment of an individual is constituted by *the characteristics of the group*. Here again a defining process related to the individual is much to the point. We may expect the leaning to conformism to be more marked where there is a considerable area of agreement between the individual and the majority in a number of important dimensions. The results of various researches back up this expectation.[4] The size of the majority would seem to be of relatively small importance. Asch had already shown in his initial study that the effect of a majority reaches its maximum with three members. Of far more importance, however, is the unanimity of the majority verdict. If that unanimity is broken by just one member, then the inclination to fall into line disappears almost completely. For this to happen the dissenting judgment does not have to tally with the view held by the "ingenuous" subject of the experiment— which would seem to indicate that the absence of unanimity in a majority creates an impression of greater tolerance towards dissentient opinion, allowing the individual to feel free to bring forward his personal viewpoint.

3. *The individual*

The results we have just been considering make it likely that *the relation between the individual and the group* is also of major importance to any explanation of conformist behaviour. Almost always, in fact, in researches done with natural groups a connection is found between the extent to which the individual conforms to the group norm and the group's attraction for the individual, where conformism is a means to obtaining sympathy.

A second aspect of the relation between the individual and the

[4] V. L. Allen, "Situational Factors in Conformity", in L. Berkowitz (ed.), *Advances in Experimental Social Psychology*, II (New York, 1965), pp. 133-75.

majority is the individual's status in the group. It is not immediately clear on intuitive grounds what kind of connection there is between this variable factor and conformism. On the one hand we may assume that the "top people" are expected to adhere more strictly to the norms and to "received opinion"; on the other hand the opposite would also seem to be justified, in that "high status" figures can allow themselves to deviate from generally accepted ideas without very much risk. As over against these expectations Homans[5] contends that people of middle status in the group will be the very ones to exhibit the greatest amount of conformity, because particularly in their case an independent view can entail a fatal loss of status.[6] To the extent that a signicant relation between conformism and social status has been demonstrated, the results support Homans, but the absence of any link in most of the studies makes one suspect that the interconnection is more complex than he supposes.

Then finally the relation between the individual and the group also finds expression in the interdependence of the group's members. In those experiments where an attempt has been made to study the effect of interdependence through a system of rewards for the group, usually a greater degree of conformism was found. What is remarkable is that rewards are generally given for *correct* replies. The paradoxical aspect of the situation, therefore, is that a person who one might suppose would try harder to make an accurate and independent judgment conforms even more to the wrong finding of the majority. One might conclude that in this situation the individual decides to go along with the majority so as not to rock the boat. But this is not a plausible explanation, because the consequence of an individual premium on independence is *more* conformism. Allen[7] accounts for this

[5] G. C. Homans, *The Human Group* (London, 1951).
[6] We find an interesting confirmation of this hypothesis in Ionesco's *Rhinoceros*. The order in which the characters in the play undergo the metamorphosis is obviously connected with their social and economic status. Boeuf and Jean, who are middle to lower class, are the first to undergo a change of appearance. After that come the principal, M. Papillon, and the logician, and finally it is the turn of Botard and the female secretary. Only Dudard, who is standing in as head, does not belong in the queue. The order is backed up by references at the "right" moments to Cardinal de Retz and the Comte de St Simon.
[7] See note 4.

seeming contradiction by postulating that the "ingenuous" subject of the experiment will take it for granted that anyone in that kind of situation has an even stronger motive for giving correct answers. For that reason he will attach more value than ever to their judgment. According to Moscovici and Faucheux[8] it is obvious what is going on here. The "ingenuous" guinea pig has even less reason than ever to suppose that the group will mislead him. Why should the majority run the risk of incurring a loss which, so far as he can see, is not going to benefit anyone?

4. *The situation*

A final situational factor of major importance to any investigation of the influence exerted by a majority on the judgment of the individual is *the way a reaction is demanded of the individual concerned*. I have put off discussing this variable until now because its significance is directly relevant to the question of what is the nature of the conduct usually described in the literature as conformism. In almost every investigation it appears that acceptance of the group verdict declines markedly where the individual does not have to make a public disclosure of his own finding. In Asch's original experiment the percentage of wrong evaluations dropped away to 12.5 per cent where the guinea pig was allowed to write down his conclusion so that the other members of the group could not discover what it was. Does this mean that the individual, when confronted with a differing verdict on the part of the majority, wants only to avoid an overt difference of opinion with the group, whereas his personal conviction is unaltered? Obviously, finding an answer to this question will have a major bearing on the significance of all inquiry into conformism and independence in the process of judgment-forming.

If we take conformism to mean a change of behaviour under the influence of a group, resulting in increased agreement between the individual and the group,[9] then we are making no distinc-

[8] S. Moscovici and C. Faucheux, "Social Influence, Conformity, Bias and the Study of Active Minorities", in L. Berkowitz (ed.), *Advances in Experimental Social Psychology*, V (New York, 1972).
[9] See note 4. W. R. Nord, "Social Exchange Theory: An Integrative Approach to Social Conformity, *Psychological Bulletin* (1969), Vol. 71, No. 3, pp. 174-208.

tion between overt behaviour and personal conviction. Conformism without a change of personal conviction and a real change of view are, however, two quite different things. We should not, for instance, expect that a behavioural change entailing no more than an overt yielding to the influence of a majority will continue when the group pressure is removed. A real change of opinion, however, will persist even when the group is no longer exerting pressure on the individual. If it makes sense to distinguish between a change in overt behaviour and a change of attitude—and there is really not much doubt about that—then the obvious thing is to ask what in each case is the difference in the significance of the factors referred to. In point of fact, not much is known about this. It would hardly seem possible to form a meaningful theory unless this distinction is at least taken into account. Asch[10] clearly recognizes this when he points out that empirical research in this field has not led to any refinement of the initial theoretical annotations. It will not suffice, he adds, to determine the quantitative relations between conditions and effects, the psychological import of which is known to us only superficially.

Conformism is not a psychological category but embraces a number of heterogeneous conditions, each of which has to be characterized in psychological terms. Tracing the social and psychological processes which underlie the tendency to conform is necessary, if we are to be able to answer the question regarding its causes.

III. THE NEGLECTED MINORITY

Most of the explanations to be found in the literature, however, do not face up to the complexity of conformism as a phenomenon. They are retrospective cost-and-benefit analyses in which the process of influencing is seen as a form of barter between the individual and the majority. The individual supplies conformity and in exchange receives social esteem, which in this line of business occupies the place of money in the economy. However,

[10] S. E. Asch, "Issues in the Study of Social Influences on Judgement", in I. A. Berg and B. M. Bass, *Conformity and Deviation* (New York, 1961), p. 143.

this one-sided account has recently been subjected to serious criticism by Moscovici and Faucheux.[11] According to them, the analysis of the processes through which influence is exerted in a social context is dominated by several assumptions—one being that the individual is regarded as a minority which merely asks itself how a difference of opinion with the majority is to be avoided and what the reward is for submission. One never, apparently, comes across the idea—so Moscovici and Faucheux argue—that the individual might be wondering how he could win over the majority to his standpoint.

Basing themselves on this line of thought, Moscovici and Faucheux arrive at a new and surprising interpretation of Asch's original research. If one sets Asch's experiment within a broader context, then the guinea pig coming into the laboratory is not just an isolated individual, but also the upholder of a general norm. He is the representative of a much bigger group in which a clear consensus exists as to which linear sections do and which do not differ in length. But in the laboratory he encounters a small group of people who consistently use a different rule for forming conclusions about linear sections. So Asch's experiment presents us not with "a minority of one against a unanimous majority" but with "a unanimous minority against a general norm". Experiments dealing with conformism serve to show not so much that the majority has power over the individual, but rather that in certain circumstances a consistent, unanimous minority can influence the general norm. For this purpose the number of people constituting the minority is relatively unimportant. The operative factor in the influencing process is the *consistency* shown by the minority. Should that minority consist of one person only, then the consistency of his behaviour at the time and under changing circumstances will affect the behaviour of the majority. If the minority consists of more than one person, then not only an individual's inner consistency but also consistency as between individuals will have a part to play. Moscovici and Faucheux have successfully confirmed this thesis in a number of experiments. It does seem, in fact, that a consistent minority can influence the majority judgment, even where an

[11] See note 8.

implicit majority-norm is present. The importance of Moscovici and Faucheux's ideas seems to me evident enough. With their analysis of the processes which social influencing entails they have exposed the one-sidedness of "conformism research". Conformism is only one of the forms in which social influence is exercised. Innovation, whereby current ideas and norms upheld by the majority are altered at the instance of a minority is the (hopeful) reverse side of the coin, which up to now has hardly been looked at.

Translated by Hubert Hoskins

Bernard Quelquejeu

Ambiguity and Contingency in the Forms of Power

ANY reflection about power—what it involves, its concrete forms and organization, its ambiguities and its specific link with history (something that can only be done very briefly here)—is faced at the very outset with two obstacles. We cannot come to any satisfactory conclusions unless these are at least partly removed.

The first has to do with terminology and is concerned with the imprecise, even equivocal nature of the vocabulary at our disposal. The second obstacle is more philosophical and is concerned with the position we take with regard to the rationality of the phenomena connected with power and the irreducibly irrational, obscure aspect of our reflection. These two questions are not independent of each other, as we shall see, and we are bound to state our attitude towards them and our choices before beginning to consider the problem of power.

I. AN AMBIGUOUS TERMINOLOGY

Anyone who approaches the subject of power will at once be struck by the uncertainty of the vocabulary employed and by the many hidden traps set by the words used to describe the phenomena encountered.

One of the most striking signs of the state of affairs is that a controversy has raged since the end of the Second World War between political scientists about its existence as a subject, the limits of its field and the definition of its methods and objectives. Not that our investigation into power should be confined from the start to *political* power alone. There are many other kinds—economic, educational, cultural and religious. Yet the hallmark of political power is that it sets forth with outstanding clarity the characteristics of all power.

One might expect that as political science is twenty-five centuries old, it could have succeeded in delimiting its field and objectives with some degree of precision and objectivity. This is, however, not the case. If the introduction of the political sciences into the university curriculum of many countries over the past twenty-five years has marked the end of a deficiency, it has in no way silenced the controversies regarding its objectives and its scientific status. Moreover, if many political theorists have noticed that, after a quarter of a century and in spite of different premises, they have in fact been exploring the same field, the debate nevertheless continues and views differ as to how political science should be defined and what categories can be used to determine its objectives.

Marcel Prélot[1] has recently been able to identify three ideas in this connection. The first is a "relational" one, which applies itself to defining a specific social relationship, distinct from other social relationships (B. Croce, C. Schmitt, P. Duclos, and in his way J. Freund). The second is a "dynamic" one, which favours the notion of power in all its most diverse aspects (H. Cook, T. Watkins, M. Weber, G. Burdeau, G. Vedel). The third idea is an "institutional" one, which looks back to the traditional concept of the State as the institution of institutions (M. Duverger, H. Maier, M. Prélot and others).

These debates clearly illustrate the uncertainties of vocabulary and the ambiguities of classification where the definition of the phenomena of political power is concerned. Should we speak of "power" (*pouvoir*) or "force" (*puissance*)? (We speak of *puissances* to describe Powers in the sense of States.) Should we speak of "domination", or of "coercion"? Should we make use of the words "force" or "violence"? Should we refer to commandment and submission or to authority and obedience? Should we locate

---

[1] *Encyclopaedia Universalis*, vol. 13, pp. 231–5, article "Politique—La science politique".

power on a scale that goes from the state of fact to that of legality? There are many other examples.

We have also to draw attention to further difficulties produced by the translation into another language of words used in an original one. The English word "power" and the French noun *pouvoir* surely do not cover the same semantic ground and cannot be considered as equivalents without grave equivocation. *Macht*, in German, has different connotations again. Does not this fact alone, namely that historically and geographically there has been and still is such variety in the terms used by men to describe the realities of power, not constitute a symptom of the diversity of the effective organizations of power and of the deep-seated historicity that affects the concrete aspects under which it appears?

This ambiguity of vocabulary ought, then, to be removed or our thinking will be too approximate. An author can, of course, define at the very outset the meanings that he intends to give to the concepts and categories that he wishes to use. A better course, however, must surely be to use categories already defined by political sociologists such as Max Weber and already offering credentials acceptable to scientific theorists. This contains presuppositions, because to define is always up to a point to make one's own, but Weber's comprehensive sociology has been sufficiently explored in its methodology and in the presuppositions of its way of understanding social phenomena (e.g., its notions of the scholar's "axiological neutrality") for it to be able to offer suitable terms of reference by which anyone can be sure of making himself understood.

So, with Max Weber, we shall agree to call "power" (*Macht*) "the chance of an individual to make his own will, at the heart of a social relationship, triumph over all resistance, without calling into question that on which this chance rests". We shall also agree to call "domination" (*Herrschaft*)—as the concrete and empirical manifestation of power—the chance of finding partners there who are ready to obey the orders given them.[2] These are both general definitions. Neither power nor domination thus de-

[2] M. Weber, *Wirtschaft und Gesellschaft* (Tübingen, 1956), I, p. 28.

fined are specific to the political scene, for there are other circumstances and other necessities in which man is brought to make his will triumph. Power can be deployed in every form of human association, be it economic, educational, cultural or religious.

Power and domination become political only when they are exercised within a delimited territory, when the will is significantly directed towards the service of the territorial group with a view to achieving an aim which has meaning only through the existence of this group and when the will is prepared to make use of *force* as a specific method, at least in the name of an *ultima ratio* when all other methods have failed. Thus the State may be defined as the political group that successfully claims to have a monopoly of legitimate physical coercion, whatever the way by which this legitimacy may be recognized (traditional, legal or charismatic domination). In the context of the above definitions, "chance"—the notion employed by Weber to indicate the probable character of every sociological construction—implies "the more or less great probability, expressible in an objective judgment of possibility, indicating that one can with good reason count on these expectations".[3]

Thus, at the basis of all domination and all power there is the fundamental relationship between commandment and obedience. If a command is executed, he who dominates possesses power, whatever may be the reasons why others submit (fear, respect, a useful purpose, opportunism, tradition, and so on). Obedience means that the partners act as if they were making the commandment into a maxim for their conduct, whatever their personal opinion may be of the value of the command as such. Power transforms the exercise of coercion into pure violence each time the subject ceases to be treated as a partner and finds himself reduced to the status of a thing. Thus understood, a commandment is by its very nature the organizational factor of the social group or political institution.

These choices in terminology are necessary so as to anchor our reflection within sociological positivity. Later on, as we advance in our research, it will be necessary to introduce other notions, in particular that of authority.

[3] *Idem, Essais sur la théorie de la science* (Paris, 1965), p. 348.

II. Power and Rationality

The other obstacle that has to be removed at the beginning of such as Talcott Parsons and Robert Dahl. Here again inconclusive ality of power. Anyone who wants to reflect about power should try to put forward the presuppositions that always govern the position that he has adopted towards the rationality of the phenomena connected with power. Reason and power, after all, are an ill-assorted pair.

One of the great achievements of Greek thought was to have brought politics into the area of philosophical speculation and to have opened the way to an understanding of man interpreted according to forms of power and especially, in this context, the State. The Greek philosophers never excluded political power from the field of the reasonable, which they explored with great boldness. They knew that, if power was withdrawn from philosophical reason, then reason itself and its claim to arrive at reality would suffer. Thinking man cannot accept a divorce between power and reason. If nothing is reasonable in the exercise of power and in the political life of men, then the politician becomes a devil and reason becomes unreal, impotent and exiled into the backwoods of the ideal. Who will then consent with any cheerfulness to a rupture of this kind, if these are the consequences? Plato understood this when he wrote: "Unless philosophers become kings in the States or those who are appointed kings become true and serious philosophers and unless we see political power and philosophy united in one and the same subject, there will be no respite from the ills that ravage the States or from those of the human race."

Yet, ever since the Greeks and especially Plato tried to justify the link between power and reason, this relationship has always been problematical. The philosopher and the politician are always in conflict. The philosopher seeks reason and dialogue, which he sets up as common arbitrator between all men. His first act is to reject violence.[4] This remains his final goal and he cannot go back on it without becoming corrupt. He aspires to

---

[4] This point is particularly developed in the works of E. Weil, notably in *Logique de la philosophie* (Paris, 1950).

the kingdom of truthful living and thus makes himself the enemy of the lie which denies and destroys relations between men.

The politician, on the other hand, has been taught by experience that truth and power cannot live side by side, because power, being born of violence, needs the support of the lie. The politician lives in a world where might has precedence over right and he well knows that history is full of the tragic ruins of cities that were led to their destruction by naïve idealists who thought they could confine themselves to trying to convince. A society policed without police exists only in utopian dreams. The exercise of power implies coercion and violence. Kant saw this when he said: "That philosophers should become kings is hardly desirable, for the possession of power irremediably corrupts free judgment." Thus everything seems to bring the philosopher and the politician into conflict. They seem unable to understand each other. The philosopher condemns the politician too often without attempting to see things from his point of view. The politician sees the philosopher as a dreamer, at best harmless but usually dangerous.

So this is the ill-assorted couple formed by power and reason. They cannot agree and yet they should not divorce. It is a good example of the contradiction that besets all reflection about power. Philosophy, which is responsible for the meaning and will of the reasonable, comes up against the meaningless and the irrational. Indeed, power is a riddle and a scandal to the rational man. Hence we perceive that any reflection about power is called upon to acknowledge the dark, irrational aspect of the manifestations of power. In the context of power, man observes aspects of himself which exhibit an enormous area of misfortune. Perhaps, in its way, this dark aspect reveals the finite character and contingency of every concrete organization of power. In any case, to think about the demons and the failures and the perversions of power is no doubt the hard but necessary path that must be followed by anyone who really wants to understand how and why power is involved in history.

III. THE DEMONS OF POWER

Few political thinkers have been as courageous and as lucid as Thomas Hobbes, who declared that it was in the political field that one of man's most basic tendencies flourished. "So that in the first place, I put for a generall inclination of all mankind, a perpetuall and restlesse desire of Power after power, that ceaseth onely in Death."[5] Right at the heart of his political thought, when he identifies man's insatiable desire for power, Hobbes also reveals the basis of his political anthropology and the problematic nature of the sacrifice that will form the creative pact of the Leviathan-State. The quotation often used to describe Hobbes's thought—*homo homini lupus*—is based on man's inexhaustible desire for power, inasmuch as it expresses man's hostility to his fellows in his struggle for life.

But the philosopher is even more lucid when he reveals the fatal workings of the appetite for power. The need to increase power, he points out, does not arise from the hope of a more intense satisfaction. Man is never satisfied, because insecurity is his lot and he can never be assured of his power or of the means at his disposal at any given moment. "And the cause of this is not always that a man hopes for a more intensive delight than he has already attained to; or that he cannot be content with a moderate power; but because he cannot assure the power and means to live well, which he hath present, without the acquisition of more."[6]

The whole of history resounds with the echoes of the ills that have been endlessly caused by the infinite evil of the desire for power. Paul Ricoeur has named "the political paradox"[7] the two facts that, while man's political life was developing a type of specific rationality which made power into a great human reality, an irreplaceable contribution to man's humanity, power was *at the same time* developing immense and specific ills, a human achievement eminently prone to evil. This is perhaps the greatest cause of misery in history. "Specific rationality and specific evil—these are the two paradoxical origins of power."

The specific evil of power has been recognized with striking unanimity. It is noteworthy that the oldest written biblical

[5] Thomas Hobbes, *Leviathan*, I, chapter 11.
[6] *Ibid*.
[7] P. Ricoeur, "Le paradoxe politique", in *Esprit* (May 1957), pp. 721–45. Reprinted in *Histoire et Vérité* (Paris, 1964), pp. 248–73.

prophecy, that of Amos,[8] denounces political crimes rather than individual faults. Over and above the survival of the outworn idea of collective sin, and before the individualization of punishment and fault, we must notice here the denunciation of the evil of power. It is the political fulfilment of man that gives to sin its historical dimension, its power of devastation. The death of Jesus, like that of Socrates, was accomplished by means of a political act.

In the *Gorgias*, Plato says basically the same thing, but in a different way. Meditating on the figure of the "tyrant", Plato reveals the underground links between power and the word—tyranny is not possible without a falsification of the word. If it is true that language is man's element, the *logos* that makes one man resemble another and is at the basis of communication, then power will be in conflict with language. It is therefore necessary to denounce the monstrous link between tyranny and sophistry: the connection between the perversion of the word and the perversion of power. In the *Gorgias*, Plato unmasked for all time the appalling potential tyrant lying in wait for the politician, the moment the latter perverts truth by hypocrisy, flattery or lies.

A final form of the evil of power (equally large and still more cunning, if this be possible) has been described with singular acumen by Marx—not only lies, but also illusion. Plato, Hobbes and many others understood that with political power they were dealing with the unique relationship of command and obedience, whence is born the need for a legal system, and they could certainly accuse historical power of being unlawful and of having discovered in rhetoric a means of creating a mask of legality. But it fell to Marx to propound the full dimension of the problem of illusion. Real power is not what it claims to be. Marx ultimately denounced an illusion, claiming that bourgeois power brought into being a State which was not man's true world, but another unreal world, which resolved real contradictions only by a fictitious law, in its turn in contradiction with real alienations. The idealism of law maintains itself, according to Marx, only through the mystifying illusion created by the cunning realism of an arbitrary bourgeois power.

Thus the demons of power never cease to divert the objectives

[8] See, for instance, Amos 1. 3–16.

of action from their rightful end. Even when everything would
suggest that the objectives of power are reasonable ones, it could
be that a fundamental irrationality is at work to make us see
them as just. The hypothesis of an evil genius is more plausible
in this area than where Descartes feared it—surely power is
haunted by a *demon* very different from the one who uses trickery
with man to turn into good the evil that he does, as Kant and
Hegel thought. On the contrary, this one turns man's aim into a
counter-aim. As Sartre said, "As human ends become realized,
they define all around them an area of counter-finality."[9]

IV. The Anarchist Claim

When we consider the demons of power, we are in danger of
becoming enclosed within a moralism that results in nihilism.
We must therefore resist the temptation of falling into two opposing types of reflection about power. On the one hand, we tend
to emphasize the lie, the violence or the illusion of power. In
this, we rely on Plato's denunciation of the *tyrant*, Machiavelli's
apologia of the *prince* and Marx's critique of *alienation*. On the
other hand, we may, with Aristotle, Rousseau and Hegel, stress
the rationality of the politician. If, in our reflection, we want to
avoid the snares both of rationalism and of moralism we must
seek out the sensible constitutive requirements of political institutions and authentic social relations, where they are concealed
in decadent forms of power which express the frenzied victory
of force.

In order to do this there is perhaps no better way than to consider the claim of anarchy.[10] This is in fact an argument which
is both irreligious and individualistic and which preaches revolt
against the dominating power in the name of a force called freedom. It is a phenomenon of primary importance in the political
history of the West.

Anarchism as a philosophical doctrine is essentially Hegelian.
Hegelianism marked the end of the movement of the philo-
sophies of the "archy" or innocent origin of man (Rousseau),

[9] J.-P. Sartre, *Critique de la raison dialectique*, I (Paris, 1960), p. 234.
[10] This is the way traced by P. Secrétan, *Autorité, pouvoir, puissance*
(Lausanne, 1969). I acknowledge my debt to this excellent book, which
has had a very direct influence on the last part of my essay.

and the beginning of an-archy. "The series of Hegel–Feuerbach–
Stirner–Bakunin is no less legitimate than the one that leads from
Hegel to Marx. It even seems . . . that the first place should be
given to anarchism. It is this that is the last stage of German
classical philosophy . . . the last possible prolongation."[11]

The anarchist position can be briefly formulated as follows.
As it reaches its goal, which is total human reconciliation, the
State (and in general all power) must be driven to its death, for
the goal in question is the giving back[12] where it belongs of the
substance by which the State is constituted—the free force of the
individual. The anarchist claim radically contests a power constituted by force in which man is less set up than made destitute,
less reconciled than alienated. On these grounds anarchy certainly
is shown to be more than a stage in thought, a necessary category
of every philosophy of power. It is precisely a negation of absolute
politics, a rejection of all power once it becomes absolute.

Certainly the anarchist claim cannot be seen as an end for our
reflection. It is by the method of going into reverse that it reveals
the excesses of a sense of a power that makes itself sacred. It is
by destructive non-submission that it contests the absolute of a
domination. Therefore it is only a stage, an awakening or a
critical vigilance. It protests that historical organizations of power
cannot lay claim to the whole of man. Reciprocity between the man
and the citizen—that is to say reconciliation of nature with history—cannot be complete. Power could never be more than a
mediation. Having been called on by the anarchist claim to recognize the limits of all power and to denounce the denials of
finitude, we must, in our reflection, make a final leap,[13] so as to
seek out the sensible requirement concealed somewhere at the
heart of the forms of power, namely, authority.

[11] H. Arvon, L'Anarchisme (Paris, 1964), p. 48.
[12] The Hegelian left ponders endlessly the question of reappropriation:
how to restore to man (Feuerbach) what he has invested in God, how to
restore to the unique and original individual (Stirner) what he has alienated in society, how to restore to the worker what has been stolen from
him by Capital (Proudhon), and how to restore to the community what
has been concentrated in the State (the anarchism or the community of
Bakunin and Kropotkin).
[13] This is the theme of the last part of P. Secrétan's book, op. cit., entitled "L'impossible absolu", pp. 155-250.

V. The Approaches to Authority

First of all we must re-examine ourselves on the subject of decision as an act of power. Does this concern the future? No, it bears on what is to come, and the difference is significant. The future can be foretold, whereas what is to come is fraught with risk. The future is an area of time when what may happen can be more or less calculated. It has to do with the idolatry of an entirely technical science of power. As for what is to come, it is an uncertain and risky projection—whereas science progresses from uncertainty to certainty, power progresses from uncertainty to decision. Power entails prudence as an indispensable expression of its finitude. Prudence is the complement of the risk which should be not only calculated but pondered on. It is the disposition to greet the unforeseeable without ever removing its gaze from the ends. Prudence is foresight, anticipation and planning, and the act of power that converts anticipation into planning, though "affected with that uncertainty as to ends which marks the breach between the order to be aimed at and the unknown to be greeted".[14]

To conclude, we must reflect again about the relationship between commandment and obedience. As soon as we recognize the ineluctable contingency of all forms of power, we are bound to ask for an obedience that is quite different from an infantile or slavish submission. Thus it is necessary, over and beyond obedience to the law and submission to man, to restore the capacity to listen, a listening that is open to what is said inasmuch as this word constitutes authority.

In authority there is something of the symbol. Just as symbolism makes one think, authority makes one act and through the action that it brings into being it aims at a meaning. Thus, if we reflect about the relationship between obedience and listening, we find that the requirement of authority is homologous with that of legitimacy in a philosophy of law. The relationship between authority and listening reveals not a political category but a category that marks the limitations of the politician. It marks the precise threshold of the region that power cannot invade

[14] *Op. cit.*, p. 208.

without making itself sacred again. The word of power therefore finds the proper delimitation of its space.

If it is true, as Plato saw, that the magic of power is transmitted through the word, then the cure for the ills of power must be found there too. The word never ceases to decline into speeches, to deteriorate into sophistry and be perverted into lies. So too does authority never cease to decline into power, deteriorate into force and be perverted into tyranny. The fact that power hence reveals itself as mediator between authority and force throws light on the ambiguity and contingency of its forms, its purely historical essence.

Translated by Barbara Wall

James Reese

The Event of Jesus—
Power in Flesh

THE New Covenant is not a book but an experience. That experience is communicated in a unique way by the compact 27-book library assembled by the primitive Christian community. This library portrays the event of Jesus as an experience of transforming power. Paul's expression of his theological summary of the experience is, "The gospel is power for salvation" (Rom. 1. 16). The community was already living out this transforming experience when Paul became a member, although he was the first to write about it. The power he experienced in the communities which he founded or visited was not an abstraction but the living Spirit of the Lord Jesus, unceasingly communicating a world of confidence and unshakable joy and thanksgiving with a sense of victory over the uncertainties and dangers threatening their members. The Spirit's powerful presence created such joy that it prevailed even in the sufferings that their new form of life necessarily brought its members. Paul could point to this joy as witness to the reality of the "power for salvation" (see 1 Thess. 5. 16; Phil. 3. 1; 4. 4).

Why do I start speaking of the event of Jesus with a reference to Paul? Because, although the primitive community's lived experience of the transforming power of God grew out of the life of Jesus as shared with his followers on earth, it did not become matter for reflection until the group felt the effects of the Spirit, whose presence produced a common life. Paul himself spoke little about the earthly life of Jesus, but he did warn members of the church at Thessalonika, "Do not quench the Spirit" (1 Thess.

40

5. 19), that living presence of gospel power. Those who accepted the transforming reality of this power and who saw it as responsible for the community's inner life and amazing growth throughout the world, made their profession of faith, "I believe that Jesus is Lord". Then they were baptized into his name, that is, into his power.

My approach to explicating this power will be: (1) to describe briefly the wider historical context of the event of Jesus; (2) to illustrate the early Christian community's experience of the power of God in Jesus; (3) to show one way this experience was expressed in the canonical gospels; (4) to conclude with remarks about how New Testament reflection on the event of Jesus provides direction for believers today.

I. THE HISTORICAL CONTEXT OF THE EVENT OF JESUS

To understand how the primitive community grew in the world and gradually achieved self-identity and became a third force in human history, it is necessary to look at the wider context in which it came into being. The historical situation of the first century A.D. was extremely complex and filled with tensions. Originally, the primitive Christians were simply part of the Jewish milieu; they cultivated Jewish values. But even here, room for diversity existed as various movements extended and modified ancient traditions. With rapid missionary preaching, the small community soon became involved in the life of the Roman Empire with its Hellenistic culture. New Testament scholarship is becoming more aware of the variety existing even in very early stages of community development.[1]

Its compact library of canonical writings yields allusions to diverse thought and ethical patterns, and reflects the impact of the contemporary religious situation on its members. The recent edition of selected essays by the eminent specialist on Hellenistic religion and early Christianity, Authur Darby Nock, preserves some of the best studies available on the world in which Jesus

[1] James M. Robinson and Helmut Koester, in *Trajectories Through Early Christianity* (Philadelphia, 1971), explore this important aspect of the early Church.

was first proclaimed.[2] His writings show that insights and values diffused by Christian preachers challenged the religious horizons and attitudes of contemporary pagan theosophists, religious thinkers who were successors to the classical and Hellenistic philosophers as civilization's spiritual leaders. I must elaborate on this point.

At the time when Jesus and his apostles were proclaiming a new presence of the God of Israel and his invitation to salvation, these pagan religious leaders were seeking salvation by means of self-sufficiency (*autarkeia*), for it put them beyond the reach of the many political, social, physical and economic uncertainties constantly threatening their life and happiness. Man had to have within himself his own source of power, either by self-acquired virtue or by a special knowledge (*gnosis*) in the form of "a vehicle of power or regeneration".[3] In the face of the failure of nerve brought on by a complex set of historical circumstances, including the spread of Oriental cults often introduced by Roman soldiers, religious experience of every variety—from sophisticated astral mysticism to the crassest forms of magic— captured the imagination of the people. In this crisis, serious thinkers turned to theosophy to find moral support in their search for salvation. As they looked to the stable divine sphere, they worshipped as gods manifestations of the variety of powers that were needed to survive in a world of constantly increasing uncertainty.

Christian preachers could neither be unaware of nor ignore the religious situation of the people to whom they preached. Only against this background can the amazing spread of the event of Jesus be understood. This point must be stressed, because New Testament commentators often limit their research to technical fields and forget that the believing community lived and changed in the open world of ongoing contact with the social life of the Roman Empire. Each year more and more is being discovered about this context of early Christianity, especially through the development of such disciplines as epigraphy and papyrology.

[2] Authur Darby Nock, *Essays on Religion and the Ancient World*, edited by Zeph Stewart (Cambridge, Mass., 1972), 2 vols.; see especially, "Early Gentile Christianity and its Hellenistic Background", upon which the following paragraphs draw.

[3] *Ibid.*, p. 61.

The Christian experience had to compete with pagan religious revivals. Eventually, it won the day because, in the words of Nock, "Christianity welcomed the sinner while paganism accepted him".[4] The power of the event of Jesus can well be described as this ability to welcome the sinner and make him feel at home. Did not Jesus invite the burdened to come to him and find refreshment (see Matt. 11. 28; Mark 2. 17 states this as his goal)? But, how is his ability to offer men comfort the working of divine power in Jesus?

II. COMMUNITY EXPERIENCE OF THE POWER OF JESUS

This article is obviously not the place to treat the hermeneutical problem of the self-understanding of Jesus, or the continuity between the earthly Jesus and the reigning Lord of the community. In one form or another, these questions arose in the primitive communities. For my purposes, it is sufficient to indicate that New Testament writers were vigorous in maintaining both the importance of the human reality of Jesus and the uniqueness of the divine Sonship he enjoyed. The community proclaimed both the incarnation of God in Jesus and the identification of this earthly Jesus with this risen Lord. Thus, Paul tells the Corinthian enthusiasts or "spirituals" that they are not speaking in the power of the Spirit if they say that the (earthly) Jesus can "go to hell" (1 Cor. 12. 3). And a generation or more later, John is still warning the church that any spirit which refuses to acknowledge Jesus is from the "antichrist" (1 John 4. 3). In other words, the believing community constantly finds its identity, role and destiny in receiving grace and freedom and the ability to believe and be saved as a gift of God in and through Jesus, for "God was in Christ reconciling the world to himself" (2 Cor. 5. 19).

If this activity of God in Jesus creates a new reality and makes the fullness of life available to humans, then identification with Jesus Christ is an integral part of experiencing God's saving power. For this reason, Paul's favourite description of the believing community is as a new creation "in Christ". Being "in Christ" was to experience of the unity of the Spirit (Eph. 4. 3) and the transforming power of the risen Lord.

[4] *Ibid.*, p. 132.

How the activity of Jesus created this unity is the theme of the famous hymn about the *kenosis* or emptying out of Jesus (Phil. 2. 5–11). Exegetes never cease returning to this piece because they find in it the most profound portrayal of the event of Jesus and the key to his power. All the energy devoted to tracing the sources of this hymn and to studying its structure and composition have not succeeded in exhausting its secrets. Here, I focus on the use of one word, *harpagmos*, the importance of which is too easily missed in the elaborate quest for literary illusions. Even the recent study of Roy W. Hooker does not explore the saving implications of this term.[5] Equally important for understanding the event of Jesus are both the meaning and the use of this rare word, never found again in Scripture. Used with the negative, it is a startling litotes, a deliberate understatement to portray the way that Jesus grasped the divine power that he shared. The hymn presents Jesus as recognizing that being on equal terms with God means in its profound dimension to be "not grasping". Thus, the self-emptying of Jesus is the revelation that to be God is to be unselfishness itself. Because he shared God's existence, Jesus knew God perfectly and mirrored him fully. In his life, then, Jesus necessarily pursued a style of service even to the act of total self-giving. He did so not simply as a model of conduct but as revealer of divine reality. Being God means being the Giver, the ever-creative author of all goodness. God can know no holding back, no selfishness, no fear of loss of power, no threat of diminished existence. For God, no dichotomy exists between creative power and saving care towards those he has made capable of enjoying his presence and friendship. Far from being isolated from mankind's needs and longings, God is powerfully involved in human destiny to the point of breaking down the barriers that enslave men. As revealer of that power, Jesus necessarily came "not to be served but to serve" (Mark 10. 45) and to give men life (John 10. 10). Since this power is eternally creative, it makes those who trust it into a "new creature" (see 2 Cor. 5. 17; Gal. 6. 15).

[5] Roy W. Hooker, "The Harpagmos Enigma: A Philological Solution", *Harvard Theological Review*, 64 (1971), pp. 95–119. A. D. Nock calls attention to references to the divinity as a prize in Hellenistic inscriptions, *op. cit.*, pp. 87, 145.

Viewed in this way, the *kenosis* hymn proves to be a revelation of what it means to be God. H. Urs von Balthasar perceived this when he wrote, "It is precisely in the Kenosis of Christ (and nowhere else) that the *inner* majesty of God's love appears, of God who 'is love' (1 John 4. 8) and 'a trinity'."[6] Further identification of the power and the unselfishness of God is made elsewhere in the community's compact library in a variety of ways. Two of these can help enrich understanding of the event of Jesus. The first is John's identification of the glorification of Jesus with his death. The word of Jesus gives life, but as the words of the cross. His willingness to offer his life for others is an effective revelation of the power of God as saving and justifying, that is, as giving ultimate meaning to human giving power (Heb. 3. 12).

The second way is the explanation of the death of Jesus in the second chapter of the Letter to the Hebrews. The author is addressing a group of Christians tempted to give up their faith in Jesus. Possibly they were former Jewish priests longing for the Jewish cult and lonely for the sense of satisfaction they felt in carrying out the prescriptions of the Law. The author offers this group a motive for perseverance by reminding them that Jesus tasted death for all—and he did this "without God", which is surely the original wording of Hebrews 2. 9, rather than the phrase found in most manuscripts, "by the grace of God". The text no doubt refers to the desolation of Jesus at his death recorded in Mark 15. 34. Having fully identified with the human condition and experienced human fear and alienation, Jesus nevertheless still trusts in God and throws himself upon the divine power by unselfishly letting go of his very life. Only in comparable trustful surrender do men experience that God's power does not crush but frees and re-creates. And so, the author warns that to reject Jesus is to cut oneself off from life-giving power (Heb. 3. 12).

No single New Testament statement or mere recollection of them is an adequate expression of the complex reality that is divine power. Yet, the celebration of that power by Jesus in emptying himself in trust is his way of revealing that divine

[6] H. Urs von Balthasar, *Love Alone* (New York, 1969).

power is saving. To experience this power is to reject other forms of salvation as capable of transforming humans and bringing them to their destiny. As 1 John 3. 14 proclaims, the presence of this power as unselfish love (*agapē*) transforms from death to life and places believers in conflict with every human attempt to manipulate reality. As part of their witness to the saving power of the Spirit of their risen Lord, leaders of the primitive Christian community felt the responsibility to communicate to new members their experience of the earthly Jesus as the locus of God's saving power. Such a task could not be accomplished by abstractions; it called for a *heiros logos*, that is, a liturgical memorial that could call the worshipping community to celebrate the event of Jesus as saving. Out of this felt need arose the unique literary form "gospel", the proclamation of the good news of experiencing God's saving power in Jesus. Without these four writings, Christianity's understanding of the reality of God and his presence in and through Jesus would be infinitely poorer. How, then, did those who had actually shared in the event of Jesus use the gospel form to convey the experience of God's saving power?

III. THE GOSPELS ON THE POWER OF JESUS

Only the Gospel of John explicitly states its purpose: "that you may believe that Jesus is the Christ, the Son of God, and that believing you may have life in his name" (John 20. 31). In a sense, this statement mirrors the underlying goal of the gospel genre. All the evangelists were concerned with the actuality of the saving power of Jesus—he is still saving those who put their trust in him. At the heart of the gospel trajectory is the new availability of God in Jesus; the final, promised, unending reign of God has begun. Jesus uncovered this new presence by word and action, specifically, in parable and in mighty deed. The parables of the reign of God are mini-dramas that portray some aspect of the mysterious working of God's power, a power at work even when men are unconscious of it (Mark 4. 26–29). The power works in a hidden way, like yeast hidden but active in a huge mass of dough until the whole is transformed (Matt. 13. 33). Thus, the parables reveal the power of God as essentially saving, and calling to conversion, and so placing hearers under judgment—not to condemn but to free. The power of God is at work when men experience conversion and new, full life.

This saving power of God in Jesus is also revealed by his miracles, again mini-dramas of the overthrow of the powers ruling this age that is passing away. This mythical world-view that provides the background for the miracles of Jesus and the context in which they were performed creates difficulties for moderns, who have a scientific view of the universe and who find little appeal in cures or exorcisms as revelations of divine power. This short article does not allow for a discussion of the hermeneutical problems involved in understanding the function of New Testament miracles which (it should be emphasized) are used with great restraint. I shall rather show the implications of three words chosen by the evangelists to describe the power of Jesus. These three words are: *sēmeion*, *exousia* and *dynamis*.

(a) *Sēmeion* or "sign" is John's favourite word to designate the manifestations of the power of Jesus, because his interest is to portray him as the revealer of the Father. John states that Jesus worked many signs (see John 2. 23; 3. 2; 6. 2, 26; 7. 31; 11. 47; 12. 37; 20. 30), and he reduces the entire ministry to a series of key signs narrated to proclaim who Jesus is. All of Jesus' signs follow the same twofold literary pattern in John: a significant deed of Jesus, followed by a discourse that transforms this deed into a revelation, an uncovering of some aspect of Jesus as God's unique Son. By this editorial process, John urges his readers on to search for the total reality of the power of God available to those who believe.

(b) *Exousia*, often translated by authority, although this is not exact, because Greek does not have a word corresponding to the legal Latin term *auctoritas*, from which is derived authority. Fundamentally, *exousia* is the ability to perform an action in the sense of not being hindered by any external force. Hence, it takes on the meaning of "capability" or "freedom". It is a key term in the Gospel of Matthew, who uses it to forge the important link between Jesus as "God with us" not only on earth but until the end of time by his powerful presence in his Church. Jesus receives the fullness of capability from his Father not simply during the period when he was visible upon earth but as the

abiding Lord to share salvation in every age. Matthew uses the
theme of the transfer of the saving power of Jesus as a literary
technique helping to structure his entire gospel. Thus, the reaction of the crowds to the Sermon on the Mount—a summary
of the fuller "justice" of the kingdom of the heavens—is to
marvel at Jesus' manner of teaching. He speaks "as one capable",
that is, one able to communicate the courage needed to live by
the saving power of God (Matt. 7. 29). Matthew begins to hint
that this power will be continuously available in the Church by
his comment at the end of his account of the healing and forgive-
ness granted to the paralytic. The people praise God "for giving
such *exousia* to *men*" (Matt. 9. 8). The phrase jolts because Jesus
alone had performed this miracle. And the shock is deliberate,
because it portrays the wonder of the primitive community at
sharing in the divine saving power of forgiving sin.

That comment also points forward to the final majestic scene
in the Gospel of Matthew when the risen Jesus assembles his
disciples in Galilee. Before giving them their apostolic commission to make disciples of all mankind, he makes a final
revelation. All *exousia* has been entrusted to him—and this implies the power to remain effectively with his followers on earth
—to make their mission possible (Matt. 28. 18–20). The similarity of this scene with that of the earlier revelation in Matt.
11. 27 shows how the transfer of power enters into the very structure of this gospel. Matthew here dramatizes the gift that the
community was conscious of possessing, a gift that Paul experienced many years before when he boasted that he and other
apostles had received *exousia* to build up the Body of Christ (see
2 Cor. 10. 8; 13. 10). I stress this point of structure because
Matthew writes not so much to inform as to build a world in
which to celebrate the event of Jesus. In that new world, the
power of Jesus is crucial, and fidelity to it is an integrating element of faith. This power is not *kratos*, brute force, a word never
used of Jesus in the gospels, but rather a liberating gift that must
be freely accepted.

(c) The third term used in the gospels to describe the power
of Jesus is *dynamis*, often in the plural, for the concrete "mighty
deeds" or "wonders" worked by Jesus as expressions of his
victory over the demonic world. New Testament writers con-

ceived the universe as inhabited by mighty beings, at times called "powers". The outpouring of the love of God "in Christ Jesus our Lord" (Rom. 8. 38–39) has stripped these powers of their control over believers. This term *dynamis*, then, recalls that the saving power of Jesus has a cosmic dimension. In this aspect, links to contemporary Hellenistic speculation are again found, for example, to the fifth chapter of the tract *On the World*. Although it is preserved with the writings of Aristotle, this is an anonymous work reflecting ideas current at the time of Jesus, and it speculates on the nature of "the power that penetrates all". Religious thinkers of the time were divided in their approach about how to deal with this power. Some proclaimed that the only hope for salvation was to surrender to it, and thus live in harmony with the universe. Others tried to escape its force by initiation into the mysteries.

IV. IMPLICATIONS OF THE EXPERIENCE OF THE POWER OF JESUS

Christianity offered citizens of the imperial Roman world another option: to call upon the name of the risen Lord Jesus and thus accept salvation as a gift of God in him. This is the power that Paul celebrates as working in his conversion, bringing him to renounce what he had previously placed his trust in and to accept Jesus as giving meaning to his life. He prays, "that I may know him and the power of his resurrection and may share his sufferings, becoming like him in his death, that if possible I may attain the resurrection from the dead" (Phil. 3. 10–11). This experience of Paul is typical of the paradoxical nature of the power of Jesus: it is always an exciting grace that combines the acknowledgment of human need with the person's total acceptance by God as his child in his Son Jesus. And so, the compact library of the primitive community still summons believers to justify their existence by embracing the reality of the love made available in the self-emptying of Jesus and in the stumblingblock of his cross (see Gal. 6. 14; Mark 8. 31–33).

From the writings left by the apostolic Church, then, emerges an amazingly consistent picture of the organic unity existing between the various trajectories interpreting the event of Jesus as they proclaim his power to the world. This power still confronts human selfishness and challenges believers to manifest by their lifestyle that God is love, and that this love never fails (see 1 Cor. 13. 8).[7]

[7] See J. P. Jossua, "L'enjeu de la recherche théologique actuelle sur le salut", *Revue des Sciences philosophiques et théologiques*, 54 (1970), pp. 24-45, for further reflections elaborating upon the divine saving power in modern situations.

Thomas McMahon

The Moral Aspects of Power

"POWER is the ability to move reality", wrote R. Guardini.[1] Ideas, values, convictions and similar elements become power only when they are integrated into the concrete life of man so that "two elements are present: real energies capable of changing the reality of things... and awareness of those energies, the will to establish specific goals and to launch and direct energies towards those goals".[2] For Guardini, the essence of power is man's intervention as agent: "Power awaits direction".[3]

These quotations from Guardini set the stage for the unfolding drama on power. Three different aspects of power will be considered in this exposition: (1) the moral determination of power; (2) the obligation to acquire power; (3) the relationship between power and justice. The Christian dimension of power will be incorporated in the appropriate places.

I. THE MORAL DETERMINATION OF POWER

The moral determination of power is a process rather than an application of general principles to particular situations. This process can be envisaged in five steps: (1) power is not a neutral force; (2) power awaits human direction; (3) human direction is given to power through decision-making; (4) decision-making is

[1] R. Guardini, *Power and Responsibility* (Chicago, 1961), p. 2.
[2] *Ibid.*
[3] *Ibid.*, p. 3.

51

effectively the exercise of power; (5) the exercise of power assumes the acquisition of power.

1. *Power is not a neutral force.* Power has been defined as "the capacity to effect change",[4] "the ability to move reality",[5] and "being, actualizing itself over against the threat of non-being".[6] An analogous term, *power* in each of these definitions relates man and his "human-ness" to others in society. Furthermore, power requires both moving and being moved towards certain goals. Direction towards goals assumes an agent who knows and wills. When the agent is human, the action becomes fundamentally human and such an action—changing the behaviour of others—becomes an observable phenomenon which cannot be even conceived merely within a strictly theoretical framework. Indeed, power can best be viewed as energy—boundless, ever-moving, constantly shifting. As an ever-changing form of energy, power becomes "human" by reason of its agent, man. In this context, power cannot be neutral; it is integral to the human act, which cannot be morally indifferent existentially.

2. *Power awaits human direction.* Guardini insists that "there is no such thing as power that, in and of itself, is valuable or significant".[7] Power exists as an observable phenomenon or fact only when someone takes and uses it. As an abstraction (i.e., a definition), power is no more than a potential fact. Power is assured existence when a human agent directs it to goals or ends. If power is to serve, it must be directed to service just like energy. Power becomes significant or valuable when a human agent directs it to service.

3. *Human direction is given to power through decision-making.* As the capacity to effect change in others, power is intimately related to the decision-making process. Decisions give direction to power. Whether a decision is made from authority, manipulation, or force, the process of decision-making does not radically differ. Weighing, evaluating and priority-setting according to a personal, functional framework are integral to each.

[4] H. Cox, "Power", *Dictionary of Christian Ethics*, p. 265.
[5] R. Guardini, *op. cit.*, p. 2.
[6] P. Tillich, *Love, Power, and Justice* (New York, 1960), p. 47. Tillich profoundly relates the ontological aspects of love, power and justice in a theoretical approach.
[7] *Op. cit.*, p. 4.

The decision-maker who directs from authority gives high priority to obedience, a condition necessary for his exercise of power. Contrariwise, the manipulator places great weight and value on the behavioural patterns of the persons he wants to manipulate; obedience would hinder his exercise of power. The decision-maker who acts from force effects change without consent of the dominated person; he consequently weighs the impact of this loss of freedom on those persons whom he has dominated. In each of these examples power is exercised through the decision-making process. The difference lies in goals and objectives which reflect differing values and priorities.

Is power a function of authority? In the ideal state, claims W. Molinski, authority "begins where it is freely recognized and ends where it becomes power".[8] Furthermore, authority is always in the service of others and their freedom. The social goal is a balance between authority and freedom so that the person and his personal values are respected. When authority is used to respect the person, it reflects God, the source of freedom and authority. Authority degrades freedom when it employs excessive power or coercion; it neglects freedom when it fails to give directives that lead to internal and external personal development. By appealing to the free assent of the subject, a person in authority does not compel; he rather appeals to a man's moral sense. Authority, consequently, is primarily a moral power or force that can effect change in others by arousing the dictates of conscience in subjects. The exercise of moral power is thus a function of authority.

The moral power that is associated with authority receives its moral specification from the power-wielder's goals; power itself has no built-in goal or direction. Furthermore, a power-wielder in authority may even use physical force to attain the common good. Physical force, like power itself, awaits human direction. When authority acts contrary to the norms of justice through excess or through defect in the exercise of physical force, the common good suffers, as the current Watergate scandals in the United States exemplify.

The Watergate scandals also reveal that the acquisition, pos-

[8] W. Molinski, "Authority", *Sacramentum Mundi*, I, p. 130.

session, or exercise of power is not always apparent in one's value system. Power-holders might deny, ignore or refuse to acknowledge their power or its effect upon others. Furthermore, the respectable mantle of authority hides the element of power more than manipulation or physical force does. Until a decision-maker acknowledges the role of power in his value system, he will be acting *with* ignorance and possibly *from* ignorance—a dangerous situation for those who suffer the consequences of his decisions. The recipients of these power-laden decisions readily acknowledge the exercise of power because it requires a change in their behaviour. Consequently, a decision-maker has a basic obligation to become sensitized to the kind, degree and impact of the power that his decisions impose on others.

4. *Decision-making is effectively the exercise of power.* Ideas have no power until they are embodied into a decision that affects others. Even a philosophy of life requires prudential judgment before it can be operative. The exercise of power (which depends upon the agent's values for direction) requires an action-oriented decision that calls upon prudence for efficient means towards an effective fulfilment of the agent's goals. Power, then, is directly involved with means as well as with goals. The selection of means is, in effect, decision-making in the practical order. Thus, it is *in actu secundo* that power becomes a reality.

5. *The exercise of power assumes the acquisition of power.* Adolf Berle claims that "power is brought into existence by the coalescence of three elements: men, a philosophy and a group capable of organization into institutions (however rudimentary)".[9] Berle suggests that the infant Church (described in Acts 1–2) is the classic example of acquiring power by the coalescence of these three elements. In addition, this coalescence achieves a "power form"—a type of *Gestalt*—which creates an overall impact upon its environment.

Before guidelines for the acquisition of power can be postulated, a few assumptions should be made. First, the acquisition of power in this section refers only to power that has an impact upon others; moral power is not considered at present. Secondly,

[9] A. Berle, *Power* (New York, 1969), p. 50. Berle has a very extensive practical exposition on power based on his experience in government, law and education. From his analysis, Berle postulates five laws on power.

the acquisition of power occasions a shifting of the *locus* of power from one person or group (*terminus a quo*) to another person or group (*terminus ad quem*); similarly, the loss of power involves the shifting of power. Thirdly, the constant shifting of power suggests the impossibility of a perfect balance or equilibrium beyond a particular instant; the human elements in power (men, philosophy, organization) constantly change and thus produce a balance of power that constantly fluctuates.

Human rights provide the basis for the acquisition of power. Freedom of association is an inherently human trait that manifests the right of persons to form a union of mutual interests directed towards a common goal or objective. The exercise of this right of freedom of association existentially establishes a power group by coalescing men, philosophy and organization. This coalescence is the genesis and consequently an initial acquisition of (social) power.

Furthermore, man has the right to use efficient means to attain his goals. The means are always sought within society, where the minimum obligation prohibits the infringing upon the rights and the exercise of the rights of others, either individual or corporate persons. The acquisition of power, thus, is intimately interrelated with free association. (When civil rulers prohibit free association, do they not effectively render their citizens powerless?) Consequently, the exercise of the right of free association implies the *right to the power* that is necessary to attain the goals of free association. The right to acquire power, therefore, has its basis in the right of freedom of association. Additionally, the acquisition of power may also be postulated as a correlative right to the right of freedom of association.

The means for acquiring power also assume a moral dimension. When means are morally indifferent, they acquire their specification from the end. Although power is morally indifferent in theory, it is not morally neutral in the concrete situation. When the end is a moral virtue—justice in this case—prudence specifies the means of acquiring power; e.g., a boycott may generally be permissible to gain a favourable labour contract. Furthermore, the means for acquiring power must be submitted to the norms of proportionality; e.g., a "wildcat" strike would not ordinarily be a proportional means if legal action or arbitration would suffice to attain a legitimate goal.

The acquisition of power, consequently, must submit to the same moral standards as the exercise of power, or decision-making: justice in all its ramifications.

II. THE OBLIGATION TO ACQUIRE POWER

The obligation to acquire power may be ascertained by answering two questions. First, do the powerful have an obligation to use their power to help the powerless? Secondly, do the powerless have an obligation to acquire power? These questions refer to the obligation of shifting the *locus* of power so that power will be more evenly distributed.

Generally speaking, the powerful have an obligation to assist the powerless. Negatively, the powerful should not infringe upon the human rights of power-seekers; e.g., civil laws which discriminate against the blacks in South Africa infringe upon the basic right of free association, equal representation, and so forth. More difficult to assess, however, is the positive obligation of the powerful to share their power with the powerless. A number of arguments can be advanced to confirm this positive obligation.

The first argument is found in the Christian goal of love. The Christian, states Karl Rahner, should use (physical) power "to bring about its own abrogation".[10] The powerful person alone has the means to effect greater balance in society; only he is in a position to assist the powerless. Christian love requires a sharing of power so the Christian goal of gradually modifying and absorbing power may be attained. Love becomes the motive for equalizing power, and (social) justice becomes the means.

That the exercise of rights are not safeguarded or guaranteed except through power is a second reason for the sharing of power. Examples abound but only one will suffice to illustrate this point. In general, capital punishment in the United States has been applied principally to the poor (and most frequently to Negroes) who could not afford to hire experienced lawyers to plead their cases. This example highlights the difference between

---

[10] K. Rahner, "The Theology of Power", *Theological Investigations*, IV (Baltimore, 1966), pp. 391–409, especially 406.

the existence of rights and their exercise. The exercise of rights depends upon a proportionate amount of power. Rahner seems to indicate the same position when he commented on the internal aspects of freedom and power: "From the Christian point of view it is not enough to say . . . that even in chains man is still free. . . . But in chains one cannot do precisely *the* definitive free act which one would otherwise have done."[11] Rahner then states that the power-holder should eliminate the results of coercive power on others and try to replace the results of power by the inner law which appeals to the person's moral sense. Freedom thus requires both an inner force (moral power) to exercise rights and elimination of external force (coercion) by the current power-holder. The elimination of power over a person occurs with the sharing of power.

A third argument stems from the notion of man's sharing in God's dominion: as God the Father shares his dominion with us, so we should share our dominion with others. Interpreting Genesis 1. 26–28, J. Milhaven claims that God made man in his image by sharing his dominion with him.[12] Guardini arrives at a similar conclusion: "Man's natural God-likeness consists in his capacity for power . . . the exercise of power is essential to his humanity."[13] Milhaven employs the analogy of a father who has entrusted his grown son with his business; the father watches the son but lets the son make all the decisions. In a similar manner, God has shared his dominion of the world with men. Thus, the "sharing" of power means the delegation of power, including accountability and responsibility. Furthermore, this sharing inevitably leads the Christian to stress positive obligations. One such obligation requires the sharing of power with others so that "others" may achieve "both the right and the obligation to rule" (to use Guardini's phrase).[14]

Like all positive obligations, the sharing of power lacks precision in determining who the referents of power might be: who must share power with whom? Obligations become vague and

[11] *Ibid.*, p. 405.
[12] J. Milhaven, *Toward a New Catholic Morality* (Garden City, N.J., 1970), especially chapter 2, "Sharing God's Dominion", pp. 29–42.
[13] R. Guardini, *op. cit.*, p. 14.
[14] *Ibid.*

confused. Priorities and needs are perceived differently by the many referents of power. What norms should guide the sharing of power?

A general norm can be postulated from the notion of biblical justice and Christian love. The Christian gives himself—and his power—by a total gift to his brothers in imitation of Christ. A more precise obligation (but still general) has been proposed by K. Davis[15] in his studies on the use of corporate power. Davis suggests two principles. The first principle balances power and responsibility: the greater the social power, the greater the obligation to use that power responsibly (i.e., in accordance with the current needs of society). An example illustrates this principle. Company ABC and Company XYZ are closing the same size factories in two different locations. Company ABC is closing its factory in a small town which depends upon the company almost totally for jobs, taxes, and its general economic well-being. Company XYZ is closing its plant in a very large city which has numerous sources for jobs, taxes, and other economic needs. All things being equal, Company ABC has a greater obligation to offset the impact of its power (e.g., by assisting employees to find jobs in other cities, by encouraging other companies to move into the small town, and so forth) than Company XYZ does.

The second principle is the "iron law of responsibility". In the long run, those who do not use their power in a manner which society considers responsible will tend to lose it. Labour-management conflicts exemplify the second principle. In refusing to treat employees in a responsible manner, business lost its power to control its labourers. Since business did not *will* to share its power with the workers, it *lost* its power through the development of a stronger, opposing power by trade unions. The *locus* of power shifted from employers to employees in many cases.

Furthermore, the two principles seem universal enough to apply to any social institution—church, government, university, union, club or family. They actually refer to the persons (sometimes covered with anonymity) within institutions: *every* person

[15] K. Davis, *Business, Society, and Environment: Social Power and Social Response*, with R. Blomstrom (New York, 2nd edn., 1971), pp. 84–98. Davis originally postulated these principles in "Understanding the Social Responsibility Puzzle", *Business Horizons* (Winter, 1967).

belongs, actively or passively, to social institutions. Everyone either possesses social power or bears the impact of social power.

The two principles may also contain a religious dimension. The Protestant ethic of stewardship, the Jewish notion of *Zedakah*, and the Catholic tradition of the social aspects of private property reflect the social power-responsibility equation. God expects the person to whom he has given more to share with the person who received less.

The iron law of responsibility restates the notion of retribution —a concept that has historically pervaded most religions of Western civilization. This notion is implicitly contained in Milhaven's analogy of shared dominion. No hair-splitting moral system, legal technicality or abdication of responsibility will justify success or failure of the father's business.

The social power-responsibility equation (positive) and the iron law of responsibility (negative) express the same notion of sharing power responsibly and somewhat refine the obligation of sharing power.

The second question raises the issue of an obligation to become powerful. The powerless may desire to avoid gaining power— after the fall man's power has been identified with violent destruction, spiritual depravity, and personal corruption of the power-holder. History is replete with examples of the devastating impact of power. But these examples generally illustrate the use of economic, social and political power; they do not reflect moral power, whereby man in general and the Christian in particular become self-actualized, fulfilled and a real being. Man does have the obligation to seek the power that will guarantee human and Christian development.

First of all, the powerless have the obligation to avoid being manipulated or dominated. The person who allows himself to be dominated might want to shirk personal responsibility and effort; he does not follow the example of Jesus whose "whole existence is a translation of power into humility".[16] True humility stems from the act whereby the Son of God became man and lived the will of the Father. The role of Jesus was that of self-renunciation of power; it was not a selfishness that refuses to

[16] R. Guardini, *op. cit.*, p. 27.

accept power and its ensuing responsibility. Jesus showed the way to Christians: he dared to be humble by freely going from lordship to slavery through a perfectly controlled self-renunciation of power. Indeed, Jesus had the "courage to be" (Tillich)—Redeemer, Saviour—through obedience to the Father. The action of Jesus contradicts the behaviour of those who refuse to be truly persons and truly Christians.

Additionally, the powerless have a strict obligation to acquire moral power because a person must have power within himself to be able to love in the first place. The Christian goal of love of self and love of neighbour—the great commandment—can only be attained when a person first of all possesses the power to love.

However, no strict obligation to seek external power can be deduced from the obligation to acquire moral power. At most, a positive obligation may be argued from the needs of society, the capacity of a person to employ power responsibly, and the limitation of other would-be power-holders. An obligation of this kind is so contingent that every general norm would be honoured by the breech.

None the less, a person may seize external power "if he sees it is being misused by others and if he feels truly creative force stirring within him".[17] The power-holder, however, realizes the "tragic nature of (physical) power, its limitations and shortsightedness".[18] Granted that physical force stems from sin (although it is not intrinsically sinful), the Christian may use it as a permissible and even necessary burden; he cannot renounce physical power without renouncing human freedom (with which it is mutually interdependent). Indeed, force is more than "an obvious existential of human existence. For it exists *either* as the embodiment of sin, egoism, rebellion against God and the worldly impatience of unbelief... *or* it exists as the effort of faith which knows that power is always unreliable and unrewarding, but accepts it obediently as a task from God, as long as he wills."[19]

How should the powerful share their power with the powerless? The answer rests upon the creativity, inventiveness and

[17] K. Rahner, *op. cit.*, pp. 407-8.
[18] *Ibid.*
[19] *Ibid.*, p. 409.

ability of the powerful to search for efficient and effective methods of fulfilment. The most obvious method is the delegation of both authority and responsibility; i.e., the granting of decision-making power to subordinates. Sharing authority reflects Christlike self-renunciation; the greater the amount and degree of sharing authority, the greater the self-renunciation. A second method assumes the validity of the statement "knowledge is power". In contemporary society where communication is almost instantaneous, knowledge becomes a source of power. The voluntary sharing of knowledge then becomes an effective method of sharing power, especially to those powerless persons who have a right to personal and social development. A third method would be realized in the application of the principle of subsidiarity, where decisions are made on the lowest practical level. Subsidiarity safeguards freedom and fosters participation in decision-making. Although subsidiarity challenges present power-holders by demanding a share in the decisions that affect a particular group, it also depends upon the permissiveness or toleration of the power-holder. Subsidiarity conforms to the notion of acquiring power through coalescence.

The real test of sharing power comes with the alleviation of conditions that have occasioned the "new powerless" in urban civilization, as victims of discrimination and other dehumanizing situations that Paul VI mentioned in his Apostolic Letter, "The Coming Eightieth" (*Octogesima Adveniens*) of 14 May 1971: "These are questions which because of their urgency, extent and complexity must in the years to come take first place among the preoccupations of Christians. ..."

III. THE RELATIONSHIP BETWEEN POWER AND JUSTICE

The most notable use of power within the Christian context can be found in the exercise of justice. Justice has for its role the recognition of human dignity through the exercise of rights. And power "guarantees" the exercise of these rights. In the traditional approach, justice requires the power to render to each person his due. In the more personalistic approach, justice needs power "to respect man's personality and to grant him what is due to him as an individual charged with the responsibility of his own destiny".[20] If the personalistic approach also includes a Christian orientation, justice, fortified by power, "requires not only new motivations, but a new dimension . . . the Christian as a Christian has rights in justice, and he can appeal to a title by claiming respect for them, the title of brother in Christ. In Christianity, the whole quality of justice is altered."[21] Both the traditional and personalistic approaches require a positive obligation to respect the dignity of others.

None the less, the question arises: How does power enter into a Christian's respect for the rights of others? The question actually raises the issue of the relationship between power and justice. This relationship will be covered in five points: (1) the need of power to effect justice; (2) the outside source of power; (3) power and justice as *ad alterum*; (4) justice as the moral determinant of power; (5) the kinds of justice determining the kinds of power.

1. From the viewpoint of the agent, justice imposes an obligation not to infringe upon the right of the other person granted by some title (life itself, the need for self-actualization, property, or the Christian imperative). Although the agent might intellectually acknowledge this obligation, he is still only intentionally just unless he has, and then employs, the power to fulfil it. The "other" has the right but he does not have the equalization of justice. Rights are not enough; man needs power to render justice. For example, the World Council of Churches recognizes the evil of apartheid in South Africa and has attempted to use its economic power to change the hiring-firing policies of international corporations, such as General Motors, Xerox, etc. The economic power of the WCC, expressed through shareholder proxies, is not sufficient to bring about an equitable change in the policies of these corporations. The imbalance of unjust discrimination still persists.

From the viewpoint of the "other", a person cannot exercise his rights without power. A black person in South Africa has the basic right to be treated with dignity. Unless he has the power to

[20] D. O'Callaghan, "The Meaning of Justice", *Moral Theology Renewed*, ed. E. McDonagh (Dublin, 1966), pp. 151–72, especially 159.
[21] *Ibid.*, pp. 167–8.

exercise this right—through legal redress in court, social mores, or force—he cannot effectively demand that others respect that right. Although power (economic, social, political, or moral) does not establish a right ("might does not make right"), it provides the energy to exercise rights and assists in establishing justice on the existential level. Through power, equality, the object of justice, is attained. Without power, rights remain *in actu primo*. Whether in the agent or in the recipient, power effects justice. This is the first point.

2. The second consideration refers to the source of power: the power to effect justice always comes from the "outside". That is, power does not come from within the person himself or even from a group itself—not from the group if it is an exercise of social justice, not from the country itself if it is an exercise of international justice, and not from the person himself but from God through the Spirit if it is an exercise of Christian justice. In a word, power is not self-generating. Economic aid to war-torn European countries provided the growth for a Common Market. Civil law was the "outside" source that granted power to labour unions and to minorities in the United States. After a revolution, a country needs recognition by "outside" sources before it can operate as an equal. The right to life of a foetus can only be exercised when the power of the State guarantees its continued existence through civil law. Even the coalescence of men, philosophy and institution contain "outside" elements, such as the freedom of association.

3. The third point recalls the social context of both justice and power. Justice is always *al alterum*. By definition, power is the capacity to effect change in others. A person cannot be just to himself; similarly, neither can a power-holder as such effect change in himself. Specifically, a power-holder cannot manipulate, force, or use authority on himself. Thus, both justice and power are relational.

4. The fourth point follows from the third: justice becomes the moral determinant of power. Power is not ethically neutral; it is always exercised within the human context. It is concerned with others and cannot exist without others; indeed, it moves and changes others. In this dynamic motion, power either re-

spects or infringes upon the rights of others. And rights are the object of justice. Power, then, receives its first moral determination when it conforms to or detracts from the standard of justice.

The exercise of power, however, falls under the decision-making steps of prudence (viz., observe, judge, act). Prudence determines the kinds of power that are necessary to effect justice in particular circumstances. Of these three steps, command (act) most effectively demonstrates the dynamism of power as it "liberates" towards the equalizing reality of justice. Thus, justice becomes the standard for judging not only the morality of power itself but also the morality of the exercise of power.

5. The fifth point applies the fourth conclusion to the different kinds of justice and power. In other words, the ends of justice—specified by commutative (exchange), distributive, legal (contributive), and social justice—provide moral standards of power. Conversely, power effects justice in its different orientations. For example, the corporate ombudsman tends to fortify the rights of customers and thereby to "equalize the relationship between buyer and seller (commutative justice). Rural groups might use their social power to demand a more equitable distribution of funds to finance higher quality educational facilities (distributive justice).

These five points demonstrate the relational aspect of both power and justice. Indeed, they show dependence of one upon the other: justice requires power for its exercise and power needs justice for moral determination. If they do exist alone, either justice will not be effected or power will not have an ethical norm for its exercise. The ancient adage "might is right" then substitutes illegitimate authority, unnecessary force, or manipulation for the balance that justice strives to achieve. When the title of rights has been manipulated, reduced, or destroyed, the power-holder has only physical force as the basis of his social relationship with others. Human dignity suffers.

When justice and power exist together, they re-create the humanizing factor of sharing God's dominion, of re-establishing balance within society, of fulfilling one's goal. The basis for this optimism is the moral power that comes from the source of all power, God the Father working through Jesus in the promise of the Spirit.

IV. CONCLUSION

How does power enter into the value system of a Christian? Both positively and negatively. Positively, power can be viewed as sharing in God's dominion whereby man, in making a decision, participates in the power of God. Christ manifested the ultimate sharing in God's power. And every Christian uniquely shares in this same power according to his particular commitment. This sharing of power also contains the moral responsibility to employ it towards humanizing and Christian purposes. The Christian should acknowledge his shared power and incorporate it into his value system. Furthermore, accountability is shared as well as power. Accountability and responsibility are proportionate to the degree of power the Christian possesses. Finally, the Christian will only effectively establish justice and fulfil the obligation of love when he has the power to fortify rights and to love.

Negatively, the Christian has the obligation of not using his power in a manner that is contrary to the norms of justice and love—manipulation, excessive force, domination. The Christian who omits the exercise of power (e.g., to permit manipulation) would be failing in his commitment to enhance the Kingdom of God through a sharing in the divine domination. (Security, as such, cannot thereby be a Christian objective; in committing himself to Jesus, a Christian risks everything and should re-live that commitment—and therefore the risk—every day.)

Even more important to the Christian viewpoint of power is the role of the Spirit. The dynamic character of the Christian life implies the necessity of power to attain its objectives. The role of directing, inspiring and orienting Christians has been traditionally ascribed to the Spirit; it is a dynamic role wherein the exercise of power is exemplified by Christian courage in the face of danger, Christian joy in the midst of sorrow, and Christian peace in the midst of turmoil. Briefly, this dynamic power gives the Christian the "courage to be". This exercise of power thus becomes a humanizing force in the world, especially in the absorbing of physical force through love.

In conclusion, power is not only ethically neutral; it can be a positive source for fulfilling Christian goals and for humanizing society by fortifying the exercise of justice and love.

Bernard Plongeron

Napoleon I and Political Ethics

ONE has only to cite certain examples of resistance to the caesaro-papism of Napoleon I to evoke scepticism from historians alive to the danger of confusion. If politico-military resistance is in question, they will draw one's attention to the insignificant and almost non-existent instances of such conspiracies after 1806. If it is ideological resistance, then they will refer contemptuously to the handful of Ideologues, holed-up in the Institut de France, whose audience was no more than a few private *salons*. If, on the other hand, one has cited the "Roman" outbursts of the clergy associated with the Concordat, one will hear of prelates torn between two allegiances: the priesthood and the Empire.

Of course it's quite amusing to indulge in ironic comment at the expense of "resisters" who did not scruple at accepting the honours, posts and awards with which a scornful Emperor bought closed lips and keys to men's consciences. The recurrence in our own times of totalitarian powers, and of instances of resistance from Bonhoeffer under Hitler to the intellectuals in the U.S.S.R. should at least have taught us that things probably weren't as simple as all that. The forms taken by dictatorships show that the awful dilemma of "obedience or resistance" has its origin in an awakening, indeed a provocation, of political ethics: a necessary factor of choice in political action.[1]

I should like to show as far as possible in the space allotted me: (1) that this political ethics continued to evolve from the time

[1] L. de Villefosse and J. Boissounouse, *L'Opposition à Napoléon I* (Paris, 1969).

of the Directory to the end of the Empire, without however modifying the course of events; (2) that it interested, upset and encouraged circles with contradictory or differing ideologies; and that it became the "location" of an (at least European) collective consciousness on which the major options of nineteenth-century society were to depend.

In order to simplify and accentuate contrasts, I shall restrict myself to the nature of a power morality among republican atheists as well as Catholics (whether monarchists or concordatists).

I. In Search of a Republican Ethics (1798–1806)

Persuaded of the death of the *Ancien Régime* which had been in its last throes in terms of political and Christian moralism, those enthusiastic individuals who "brought about" the events of 1789 were relegated, bitter and disturbed, after the revolutionary venture, to the icy solitude of the academic discussions of the Institut. The members of the moral and political science seminar tried to draw the lesson of their error: having started out with the intention of endowing Europe with the Declaration of the Rights of Man, the charter of all freedoms, in 1793 they encountered Robespierre, then the Terror, violence and dictatorship—formal contraries of a political morality.

More than one of them shared the opinion that their colleague Volney dared to put into writing: "Our masters taught us not to doubt in any way ... but as experience reformed my education, I saw that I just had to renounce that formal inclination; and if any doctrine remained for me to follow and to preach it was that of greatly doubting. . . . To use Sieyès' expression, I am of the party of facts." Atheists more in method than by conviction, these "supporters of the fact" hoped again, after the 9th Thermidor, for the possibility of building a just, free and fraternal society. Henceforth they were to be concerned with the development of what they themselves called "social science", for the purposes of a republic whose guarantor might well be Bonaparte.

What was the nerve-centre of that social science to be? What would be the basis of the institutions that would evolve from it? That was the dual question which absorbed the members of the seminar of moral and political sciences throughout the year VI

(1798). Accordingly they set as a theme for examination: "What are the most appropriate means upon which to base a nation's morals?" The Abbé Gregoire, a member of the seminar, opened with a precise response in his paper: "It belongs above all to education to ensure that all the branches of the political tree are fed by this precious juice, this collection of maxims which have most improperly been called *republican morals*. Is it possible to conceive a *non*-republican morality?" The Abbé had no difficulty in proving his thesis, thanks to Montesquieu: "Since virtue is the incentive of republics and virtue calls itself love of one's country, it follows on the one hand that virtue and the republic are only one and the same thing, and on the other hand that the complement of all virtue is patriotism." Unfortunately, after the onset of the dictatorship of the Mountain, liberals had good reason to distrust patriotism as the mainspring of a political ethics.

Their enemies, the ultramontane Catholics, exploited this difficulty and triumphed at small cost: for surely a morality defined in this way was virtually contingent. That enthusiastic polemicist, the Abbé de Boulogne, put it thus (ironically): "Are we to think that morality depends on the caprice of legislators; that they can discuss and settle it by a mere show of hands; that it is up to them to bend it to our institutions, instead of bending our institutions to it; that what was moral yesterday can cease to be so today, and that what is moral today can cease to be so tomorrow?"[2]

In the form of the respectable Catholic objection to a situation ethics, the future bishop of Troyes had posed the basic question: instead of discussing the *means* of a republican morality, he set forth its *basis* for us: "Is it the constitution [of Year III of the Revolution]? But a constitution is all the more removed from being itself an ethic the more it takes an ethic for granted." He rejected the possibility of taking the preamble to the Constitution or the Declaration of the Rights of Man as a moral philosophy, for the reason that all the relations therein defined (liberty, equality, duties of fathers, of sons, of husbands and wives, of citizens, and so on) "existed before there were any republics".

[2] The *Oeuvres* of M. de Boulogne; *Mélanges* (1827), vol. 2, pp. 215–16 (article of 1799).

The members of the Institut were so concerned with the difficulty of *grounding* a republican ethics that they decided to offer it as a subject for competitive discussion in 1798. They hoped that the following question would elicit the desired response: "What are the most appropriate means for grounding the morality of a nation?" None of the nine papers presented was chosen for an award. Consequently they altered the subject. Instead of "What are the means?" the Institut asked "What are the institutions?" The eight papers selected showed that the subject was the more difficult because too restricted. In January 1800, for the third time, the Institut started the debate again, after having proposed a plan for the candidates. Among the best contributions was that of J. B. Say, the economist. He published it under the title *Olbie, or an Essay on the Means of Reforming the Behaviour of a Nation*.

But this time the discussion centred on the quasi-impossibility of any agreement on the word "grounding" a morality. Some thought they could detect a *petitio principi*: if one is to suppose that a Constitution exists which accords with morality, then the bases of morality are grounded and known. The quiet courage of Bernardin de Saint-Pierre was needed to break the circle. Given the task in the year III of producing a manual of republican morality, the famous author of *Paul et Virginie* was appointed minute-secretary for the third *concours*. He explained to his colleagues that some defined morality in terms of its effects, whereas other invoked education, and yet others laws. The last-named invented a morality grounded on feasts and patriotic spectacles, when others had located it "in our own eminently versatile heart. But the basis is in God, the author of the pre-eminently regular laws of nature from which we derive our moral bases". The secretary developed this proposition at length before an audience too astonished to show even a trace of outrage.[3] Louis-Claude de Saint-Martin, the unknown philosopher who had competed for the prize, had previously been entirely of the same opinion as Bernardin de Saint-Pierre: "Therefore it is not a question of foundering in the relativism of a morality which could fit only a republican government, as would seem to be indicated by the

[3] Bernardin de Saint-Pierre, *De la nature de la morale* (Paris, year VIII).

Institut's project, but of finding the bases of theoretical morals which could inspire and enlighten all practical institutions under any government. That is a sublime point that no human legislator could reach without himself being aflame with the 'spirit of life' (we do not mention the name of God), which is capable of reinvigorating, purifying and grounding all human moralities."

Naturally the atheists of the Institut could not bow to any such "reactionary" conclusion. But that did not prevent the moral consciousness of the Ideologues experiencing a reflux of encouragement, rigour and elevation. Since no satisfactory solution could be found to the problem that had been posed for a period of three years, the Ideologues set themselves henceforth the task of designing a kind of anti-Machiavellianism (Machiavelli is often referred to in subsequent texts and associated with Robespierre). This was their form of ethical opposition to Napoleon. By "ethics" we may understand a faithfulness to those liberal principles which forbid the use of absolutely any means of feeding political resistance; for that would be to revive Machiavelli and to use the same weapons as Napoleon—mainly force, physical violence and ideological oppression.

On behalf of this liberal and firmly republican ethics, the Comte de Toulongeon described to the Institut in 1803 the desired positive nature of the opposition: "This trend to opposition tends to national pride and is more worthwhile than indifference. The latter leaves everything to be done, whereas the other only forbids that everything should be done. Hence the spirit of opposition comprises an integral part of the public spirit; it is the acid which prevents the alkalization of the humours in the body politic."[4]

But, rather than accept this neat and beneficent solution for the public spirit, the new Machiavelli marked his reign with a series of increasingly dictatorial measures; discouragement was in store for the old republicans, despite their imperturability in the fastness of a lonely liberalism. The most famous of them, Destutt de Tracy, continued the struggle with the publication of his *Commentary on the Spirit of Laws*, written in 1806–7. Fiercely

[4] *De l'esprit public: Mémoires de l'Institut de France* (1804), vol. 5, pp. 234–5.

defending the freedom of mind and tolerance, he saw the Concordat as "profoundly immoral", inasmuch as "any government which wants to indulge in oppression gets the priests in tow and then tries to make them powerful enough to serve its purposes". This was a strong echo of the statement of his colleague in the Institut, J. de Sales: "The inward harmony of a Republic depends on the way in which it applies ethics to its politics and to its religion."

II. Against the "Usurper"—the Royalist Clergy

Even though the thirty bishops of the *Ancien Régime* who were living in exile in London and in Germany refused to subscribe to that kind of sentiment, their primary reason was surely its dependence on a republican principle; yet they also rejected it because it distinguished between morality, politics and religion. In fact they refused to accept the Concordat on the ground that by it the Pope ratified this kind of distinction, the product of an atheistic government. But did they stop short at summoning the faithful of their former dioceses to total resistance to Rome and to Caesar? Certainly Napoleon showed that he was more irritated than disturbed by this dissidence on the part of the "Petite Eglise" which was nurtured right up to the twentieth century by Christians in various areas of France.

For these anti-Concordatarians, political morality was involved in a true politics drawn from Holy Writ which alone justified that *Declaration of the Rights of the Monarch* (1801) by virtue of which the bishops stigmatized the imperial regime. Louis XVIII was the embodiment of legitimate power, even though he was not a consecrated king. Their whole ethical resistance was summed up in the theological distinction between fact and right. "It is possible", declared the bishops in council in London, "that the new order of things [the Empire] may to some extent cite the weight of those disasters under which anarchy made the people groan, but it will satisfy neither God nor Caesar, because, rejecting divine precept [they had previously emphasized the difference between advice and precept], that which is due to Caesar is not rendered unto Caesar. This new form of government bears on its forehead the brand of iniquity, by virtue of the very fact that it excludes the legitimate ruler, and this hateful mark is visible to all watchful eyes."

Hence Napoleon became the Beast of the Book of Revelation, and to resist him became a religious duty. But we still have to explain why. The power of the new Caesar, even though crowned at Notre Dame by Pope Pius VII, "is only a factual power and not a power as of right; in addition it relies only on possession or rather usurpation; but the sceptre still belongs to the legitimate ruler; even though the actual exercise of authority is in other hands, the legitimate ruler continues to hold all rights, even though he may be forced to suspend their exercise. Thus Joash escaped the anger of Athaliah and, hidden in the temple by instruction of Jehosheba, maintained while there, throughout the tyrannical rule of a degenerate queen, the right he enjoyed to the throne of David."

The notion of sacrilege, clearly established, became the ethical mainspring of a movement of resistance to usurpation. Simultaneously, it effaced any scruples which might have been based on a sensitive exegesis of Romans 13: "For there is no power but of God. . . . Whosoever therefore resisteth the power, resisteth the ordinance of God." The objection of a possible assent to the "authority" of Napoleon was removed in advance since the bishops had concluded that the imperial Beast could in no case possess the least fragment of authority, for Louis XVIII was alive. Since the Emperor was taken as a tyrant, according to the Thomist thesis, it was logical that the bishops should at least imply that justice should be done. That had already been the supposition of the Vendéens when they made their attack in the rue Saint-Nicaise during the First Consulate. But in this case the bishops omitted to call upon their faithful to restore justice in France in this way; they did not preach sedition.

Curiously it was in the writings of the economist J. B. Say, "forbidden" by the Emperor, that the full development of this royalist "ethics"[5] was to be found: "It has been said that the power of kings is from God because God allowed them to reign. But from that which God permits we are not entitled to conclude that he ordains. Otherwise he would have ordained that Nero

---

[5] *Sur l'autorité divine des rois* (c. 1813; Bibliothèque Municipale de Besançon, ms 1442, fol. 354).

should order his mother's death and that Caligula should appoint his horse a Roman consul. If God authorizes a bad prince by the sole fact that the prince succeeds in his usurpation, he authorizes me to conspire against him and to topple him from his throne from the moment when I can do that successfully. My loyalty is no more a duty than his good behaviour, and it is quite idiotic to teach that I should respect his weaknesses and serve his desires when I can free myself from them."

A tough lesson in moral theology from a "republican" who lay low under the Empire. Rather than the bishops of the "Petite Eglise" it was the prelates of the Concordat who were impressed by it, and who were able to put it into practice, at least in two cases which proved to be decisive for the future of the imperial regime: the publication of the imperial catechism in 1806, and the national conscription on behalf of a "just" war which Napoleon had to undertake against the coalition powers.

III. POLITICAL SUBMISSION AND THEOLOGICAL RESISTANCE

The Napoleonic bishops were no more than "prefects in purple" and his salaried clergy loud-speakers for the bulletins of the Grande Armée. Looking more closely into the matter, it is clear that the imperial cult evoked a dual political dialectic: that of the social order (the public) and that of (private) opinion, to use Freund's valuable distinction.[6] The existence of one commandment challenged by that of obedience determined the dialectic of the social order. In our historical perspective, that social order was characterized by duties towards the Emperor, laid down in the imperial catechism (1806) and by duties towards the fatherland, more or less identified with Napoleon; the latter posed the major problem of the "just" war by the indirect route of conscription. This first dialectic of the social order in fact depends on a second: opinion. To the extent that the latter approves, jibs at, criticizes or resists the command, obedience is transformed, adulterated and even destroyed.

Let us look at the consequences of the foregoing in terms of two moments of the Empire. In 1806 power could consider itself master of opinion; the social order ruled. It was the right moment

[6] J. Freund, *L'essence du politique* (Paris, 1965).

to promulgate the famous *Catéchisme impérial*. In 1808 the Empire was threatened by war; "opinion" steadied, hardened and murmured against the warlike moves of an Emperor who was tearing young citizens from their homes in order to "defend France" against the coalition powers. In both cases the clergy had to take sides: the Emperor required them to do so, and the faithful expected it. What were those bishops to do whose status as high ecclesiastical functionaries obliged them always to ratify the dialectic of the established social order, but whose theological awareness could push the dialectic of "opinion" in the opposite direction?

Without going into detail,[7] we must remember that the *Journal de l'Empire* of 5 May 1806 uncompromisingly revealed the existence of an imperial decree on the publication of a catechism (the only one henceforth to be used in the parishes of the Empire) in the first fortnight of August. No member of the French episcopate had been consulted in the preparation of this catechism. Admittedly it was said to be a replica of the *Catéchisme de Meaux*, already composed by Bossuet, except that in 1686 a single lesson sufficed for the fourth, fifth, sixth and ninth commandments. In 1806, Lesson VII, "Suite du quatrième commandement", complaisantly outlined the matter uncompromisingly summarized in the second part: "*Question:* What are we to think of those who are inadequate in their duties towards our Emperor?— *Answer:* According to the apostle Paul, they oppose the order established by God himself and render themselves worthy of eternal damnation."

There was mixed astonishment and consternation in the bishops' palaces on reading this surprising exegesis of Romans 13. Most of the bishops decided on passive resistance. On the most varied pretexts, they delayed the publication of the catechism, and the end of the Empire put a stop to this excess. But others put pressure on the Minister for Religion in order to have the unfortunate Lesson VII revised. The closer they were to the seat of power, the more directly they spoke their opinion. This is clearly shown in a private correspondence between Archbishop de Barral

[7] For this section, see my *Théologie et Politique au siècle des lumières, 1770–1820* (Geneva, 1973), pp. 279–93.

of Tours and his minister Portalis. De Barral was one of the two ecclesiastical negotiators sent to Pius VII in Savona in order to bend him to obey the orders of Caesar. Instead of using his considerable political credit to organize "opinion", Barral quietly redressed the social order: to speak of "eternal damnation" was not only a theological incongruity but a major political ineptitude. That kind of threat would only awaken a resistance to power, whereas the passage, according to the Pauline precept, in positive terms of an obedience required not by fear but by "love", both re-established Christian morality and advantageously served the interests of the Sovereign. Despite the unrelenting irony of his minister, the highly imperial Barral "liberated" his theological resistance: "You wish to use religion to maintain the respect due to the ruler's authority and you have the right to do so. But let religion speak its own simple, unified language; let St Paul say what he did say and don't make him say something he didn't say. He knew how to evoke men's interest in the hidden folds of the human heart. . . ."

This theological resistance was all the more absolute inasmuch it did not put "order" in question, for it was a matter of *private* interventions of which the inhabitants of the diocese of Tours were not always aware. It was a resistance that deepened, and came to include all political morality, as if it were drawing strength from its own interior logic when it was a question of "blessing" war.

This time Barral showed anger (and a few other bishops followed him) at the ministerial injunctions. He criticized his episcopal colleagues who depicted conscription in a scandalously idyllic manner. Without wishing to censure them, he asked "them, and the Government, to excuse me if I have looked upon such direct and impolitic addresses on their part which would sound better from the lips of a Prefect, a Mayor or a Recruiting Officer than from those of a Bishop or any other pastor of souls".

Hence pastoral resistance joined political resistance, arising from the deliberations of the members of the Institut. Practical impotence to correct the Napoleonic trajectory did not confine them to complete silence. On behalf of the gradual restoration of a political ethics calling in question the legitimacy of power (usurpation), it had been possible to discern the *means* of grounding a power. This meant a return to the preoccupations of the seminar for moral and political sciences of 1798.

Henceforth Europe would be warned whenever there was any pretence of dictating in the name of a "legal order". As the extremely conformist *Journal Ecclésiastique* put it in May 1829, the legal order will never be anything other than what human laws make it. But are not laws exposed to the prejudices, vices and caprices of the lawmakers?: "Laws do not make manners. But manners certainly give rise to laws and, consequently, make them good or bad. Therefore it is to the social order and the moral order that one should adhere primarily as the true bases of the legal order." Why? Because the socio-moral order "tends to repress all vices which are injurious to society and to cause to be practised all those virtues which are capable of maintaining and preserving it". This conclusion would have pleased the republican Ideologues immensely; for a long time it was to define the character of European liberalism in the face of any totalitarian enterprise.

Translated by John Griffiths

Claude Gerest

The Spirituality of Authority in the Eleventh and Twelfth Centuries

THE historian who is looking for a spirituality of authority taken to its furthest limits quite naturally turns to the eleventh and twelfth centuries. In this period the problem of authority, in the sense of that of the source of political and ecclesiastical powers and their legitimacy, appeared in its sharpest form. It was involved in the disputes between sovereignty and prelates, which culminated in that between emperors and popes (the investiture dispute, 1048–1122; the struggle for the *dominium mundi*, 1157–1197). Also relevant is the background of feudal anarchy, anarchy from above, if you like, which was still very strong at the beginning of the eleventh century and made the desire for an indisputable and sovereign judgment more urgent.

At the time the few conceptual instruments available to solve a problem which was simultaneously theoretical and practical were all ecclesiastical. Canon law based on decretals and conciliar decrees and a political theology deriving from St Augustine's *City of God* were the weapons of both imperial and papal publicists. At any other time, such weapons would have been useless. In the Middle Ages they were effective within a spirituality which was widely accepted by society. Men lived at that time in a world in which visible realities were valued as symbols and emanations of a "heavenly" reality. This vision, better expressed in art than philosophy, is the joint product of Christianity and of the neo-Platonism represented by Denys and Duns Scotus. Contemplation of a higher harmony interferes with the struggle for a better historical state of Christianity. It is easy to see how, in this system of symbolic references, it was above all those who exercised authority who were spiritualized (placed in relation to a higher, invisible power). A modern critical attitude will dismiss this as a projection on to a mythical field of earthly realities experienced or desired. This is no doubt true, but it does not follow that study of the double movement from the figure to the transcendent sphere and from that sphere to the "sacralized" figure can be reduced to that hasty dismissal. The spiritual aura surrounding the origin and exercise of power in the eleventh and twelfth centuries is richer in meanings than one might think at first. Its expression was always restricted by an element of contradiction, not only because holders of authority were well able to criticize the excessive sacralization of a rival authority, but also because the Christian reference made it impossible ever to lose sight completely of the gospel paradox of the Master become servant and power denying its dominative dimension.

At a time when Church and civil society lived by the same universal force, three great figures above all were the basis for contemplation of the mystery of authority, the emperor, the pope and the secular priest. The least religious of the three was probably not the emperor.

I. The Imperial Christ and the Vicissitudes of his Image

Around the year 1000 the empire had once more become the great institution of Western Christianity. The house of Saxony, in the person of Otto I, had restored it (962) and given it a solid territorial base in control of Germany, Italy and Burgundy. Thanks to him the pagan invaders had been reduced to impotence and Christian missionary activity was protected among the Slavs and Hungarians.

The authority of the imperial figure was that of a successful war leader, and that of the heir, through Charlemagne, Constantine and Augustus, of the Roman tradition and its immemorial rights. This explains why the emperor was chosen from a vigorous race (the Franks and then the Saxons) and then crowned at Rome and acclaimed by the Roman people. But force alone was not enough for a world which wanted to see itself in terms of legitimacy, justice and the unions of souls, and political thought, in spite of the memories of Rome, was short-term. This meant that the clergy, who had preserved the imperial ideal and passed it on to the people through the liturgy and teaching, had no difficulty in transforming it into an ideal of Christianity, both at the time of Charlemagne and at that of the Saxon restoration. The emperor ruled the "Christian people"; he was responsible for the churches, at least for their orthodoxy. If he did not himself have priestly powers, his authority watched over the permanence and dignity of the order of priests.

As a figure within the Christian Church, its minister, the emperor was not measured solely by criteria of his utility—to stay too long on a functional level was contrary to the spirit of the age. He was a sacrament, the emanation of a power from above, a figure of Christ. He was not directly a figure of Jesus the Christ, but of those who in the saving history of humanity had prefigured his role of unifier of peoples and liberator, and had thus manifested the power of God. Otto was a messiah like Cyrus. In him God was revealed as master of history. "Iron Babylon and Golden Greece fear great Otto and serve him with bent backs. He whom the King of Kings has freed rules the whole world as emperor," were the words with which Otto of Vercelli greeted Otto III on his entry into Rome in 998, and he added—thus connecting the actions of the emperor to the struggle against the forces of evil until the *parousia*—"You two lights" (he was also addressing Pope Gregory, the cousin and protégé of the emperor), throughout the world shine in the churches and put darkness to flight."[1] This vision of the emperor as anointed by God to fight his battles had a new period of vigour in the eleventh century. To explain and justify the appropriation by the Saxons of Charlemagne's crown a sort of theology of history was invoked which was more or less based on chapter 7 of Daniel. The empire or *regnum* (in the sense of supreme legitimate rule) was regarded as one through the ages, a gift of God for the accomplishment of his designs. God bestowed this unique gift on different peoples in turn according to their respective merits and the possibility of making it fruitful. This was how

[1] Poem by the bishop Otto of Vercelli addressed to Gregory V and Otto II in 998; quoted in Schramm, *Kaiser, Rom und Renovation*, III, p. 62, and Folz, *L'idée d'Empire*, p. 200.

the empire passed from the Assyrians to the Macedonians, then to the Romans, and from them to the Franks and the Saxons.[2] The choice of a person to be emperor was therefore the highest revelation of the finger of God in the human adventure leading to the *parousia*. This choice was symbolized by the anointing which made man's chosen a "Christ" of God. "The man who is drenched by this symbolic dew can boast of a heavenly anointing", wrote Peter Damian on the eve of the investiture conflict.[3] The same writer included this anointing in the twelve "sacraments" he recognized. This ascetic with no worldly interests was neither toadying nor playing politics; he was merely a representative of one of the most traditional forms of the mystique of the emperor.

However much the Old Testament had influenced his image, the imperial Christ, ruling the "Christian people", placed his authority at the service of the aims of the New Covenant. He was expected above all to bring "justice and peace". These two key themes of the *City of God* had dominated the Carolingian restoration, and they were still being used to justify the imperial cause in the struggle against the eleventh-century popes. The justice and peace considered here have more to do with entry into the harmonious world of the last times than with particular ethical values: a monarch who wages war does not thereby lose his right to the title "peace-loving". In addition to this eschatological reference, imperial authority was expected to assume strictly evangelical aspects. Mercy, patience and concern for the poor were its characteristics just as much as majesty. Alcuin had addressed Charlemagne as "avenger of crimes, guide of the wayward, consoler of the afflicted, support of the good".[4]

[2] This idea of the *translatio imperii* to the most worthy peoples is attested in the Othonian period by Folcuin, abbot of Lobbes (*Gesta abbatum lobiensium*), the nun Hrotswitha (*Gesta Oddonis*), Jean de Viktring (*libri certarum historiarum*) and the translation of Boethius by Notker of Saint-Gall. Cf. van der Baar, *Die kirchliche Lehre der "translatio imperii"* (Rome, 1956).

[3] Cf. Peter Damian, "Sermo 69", Migne, *PL*, CXLIV, 899. The author defends the old Carolingian thesis of Christendom guided by the emperor and the pope in connection with the German court's settlement of the dispute between Alexander II and the anti-pope Cadalus.

[4] Letter *Domino pacifico David regi*, June 799 (i.e., before the imperial coronation, but fixing the image of sovereign authority), *Monumenta Germaniae Historiae, Epistolae*, vol. IV, No. 174.

In a very special way, the Holy Roman Emperor was expected to symbolize and maintain the unity and universality of the Christian people. In the eleventh century, he was to be judged as having failed in this task because France, England and other Western kingdoms had withdrawn from his authority, while Byzantium still claimed to be the only authentic seat of the *Basileus* of the Romans. Nevertheless, the force of the universal vision was such that, even in this age of divisions, the emperor was still regarded by his supporters as not just a German ruler, but the supreme leader of Christendom. It was he, more than the pope or in equality with him ("the two eyes of the head"), allowed the Church to present itself as the united body of Christ. According to Otto of Freysing in the time of Frederick Barbarossa, the existence of Christian emperors guaranteed the uniqueness of the *City of God*. This view was part of the Carolingian tradition, expressed in particular by Agobard, bishop of Lyons, according to which the rule of one emperor was the political translation of Paul's mystical body.[5]

In the medieval West, the emperor was not thought of as a directly paternal figure. He was rather a recapitulative one (a little like Jesus in the redemption), enabling Christian men to live as obedient sons (gathered together in the person of the emperor, who was obedient to God). In this way, if there were hesitations about identifying the emperor with Jesus the Christ, there was great similarity between him and the imperial Christ. Were not both a "reflection of the glory of the Father" (cf. Heb. 1. 3)? This is no doubt what Otto III wanted to imply when he had scenes from Revelation embroidered on his coronation robe, from the book in which the saviour of the gospels is connected with Daniel's Christ. It was said most clearly by Benzo of Alba, one of Henry IV's defenders against Gregory VII, in his *ad Heinricum* of 1068: "God goes before his Christ to prepare for him a mass of victories. The whole earth waits for him as its saviour, and the crowd goes out to meet him with palms and branches, and opens the gate of the city to him. Before the face of Augustus the pride of rebels breaks like a straw. Let all Christendom praise the creator who makes enemy attacks fall

[5] Cf. Bressolles, *Saint Agobard évêque de Lyon* (Paris, 1949). For Otto of Freysing, cf. *Chronica Lib.* V, prol. ed. Hofmeister, p. 228.

back before the eagles of the Most Christian Emperor.... Vicar of the creator, the favour of God has raised you to a sublime height and placed you above all powers and laws and all kingdoms.... My prayer is that the emperor will direct his thoughts towards God, and I give honour and glory to Him who has created, in the midst of human creatures, another creature in his own likeness."[6] It is true that such extravagant periods, thrown into the middle of a controversy, do not sum up the political thought of the whole period, but they are nevertheless the final stage of a deeply rooted imperial mystique.

If an aspect of the glory of Christ and his rule can be seen through the emperor, it ought to follow that Christ was in some way regarded as emperor. The eleventh century believed this and Romanesque art expressed it, though less systematically than the Byzantine. In the twelfth century Christ was declared in sermons to be king both by birth (the hypostatic union) and by conquest (his fight against Satan). Matthew's account of Jesus' entry into Jerusalem, together with the prophecy of Zechariah, "Lo, your king comes to you", was a fundamental text, and we have seen its influence in Benzo of Alba's image of the "imperial Christ". The authors of the sermons were not adopting the imperial cause, but they did see the Saviour in the role of supreme leader, warrior and peacemaker of Christendom. Whereas today we find it hard to give any acceptable meaning to the title of king given to Jesus, the whole difficulty for the Middle Ages was to explain why the kingly Jesus had made so little use of his royal power in temporal matters. Those interested in knowing more about this idea of the kingship of Christ should consult Dom Leclerq's very accessible book on the subject.[7] This author has shown very clearly how political practice in its turn influenced religious imagery.

Nevertheless, although the theme of Christ the king dominates the pious literature of the twelfth, and still more of the thirteenth century, the image of the imperial Christ as applied to earthly rulers was challenged. It was challenged by the sup-

[6] Quoted from Folz, *L'idée d'Empire*, pp. 206–7.
[7] Dom Leclerq, *L'idée de la royauté du Christ au Moyen-Age* (Paris, 1959), especially pp. 110 ff.

porters of the pope. Some of them did not stop at asserting the supremacy of the "spiritual", but embarked on a demystifying analysis of temporal authority. Without denying a divine origin of power in some sense, Manegold von Lautenbach, writing in 1085, based the sovereignty of emperors and kings on a contract between them and the people. This contract required the ruler to perform specified services, and the role of the ecclesiastical power was to intervene if these services were not performed.[8] In this way, curiously, at the end of the eleventh century it was theologians and canonists who took the first steps in a movement to secularize political thought. Among the supporters of the emperor some, such as Otto of Freysing, continued to put forward the Carolingian mystique of the emperor, while others found a new base for their cause in a return to the Roman law of antiquity and its secular conception of power. Peter Crassus was the head of this new school of jurists, which had its centre in Bologna. This school came to conceive of secular authority, not as within the Church, but as above it, though this view was not clearly expressed until Marsilius of Padua. The courts of the new monarchies of France and England also displayed this double tendency to place the monarch at the head of the Christian sacred order or to practice, to the advantage of the civil authority, thus making a clear distinction between the sacred and the profane spheres.[9]

II. PAPAL DOMINATION AND SPIRITUAL RULE

During the first half of the eleventh century, the pope, unlike the emperor, had no prestige, few powers, little moral reputation and no chance of success in reforming the Church. The throne of Peter was occupied, after a succession of profiteering and intriguing representatives of the nobility of the Latium, by a line

[8] Cf. Manegold de Lautenbach, *Liber ad Gebehardum, Mon. Ger. His., Libelle de lite*, I, pp. 308 ff.
[9] On the conception of imperial authority, cf. Folz, *L'idée d'empire en occident du Ve au XIVe siècle* (Paris, 1953), G. de Lagarde, *La naissance de l'esprit laïque au déclin du Moyen-Âge* (mainly about Ockham and Marsilius of Padua), I (a survey of the thirteenth century) (Louvain and Paris, 1956), Fliche, *Le Réforme grégorienne*, III (the anti-Gregorians) (Louvain and Paris, 1937); Arquillière, *Augustinisme politique* (Paris, 1955).

of honest officials protected by the German court and dependent upon it. The situation changed in 1048, when Henry III deposed three competitors for the triple crown and imposed his own candidate. This pope, Leo IX, proved himself a thorough reformer and was followed by a line of successors worthy of him which stretched up to and beyond the investiture controversy. The popes took in hand the renewal of Christian society and freed ecclesiastical offices from the grip of lay lords. In order to achieve these aims they had to take over power in Christendom, force emperors and kings to back down, direct crusades in Spain and the Holy Land and build up the most centralized administration in the West.

This was the "papal theocracy". There is no need here to go into the details of the politico-theological views which lay behind it. With regard to the powers, the distinction between temporal and spiritual power continued to operate, but, by virtue of his responsibility to all Christians and his duty to guide them towards ultimate salvation, the pope alone, at least in the eyes of his supporters, possessed supreme authority. This gave him the right to intervene in every sphere and to depose princes to the extent that this was relevant to his universal mission (and he was the sole judge of the limits of his competence). In short, the popes of the end of the eleventh century and of the twelfth century regarded themselves as emperors, supreme judges at the summit of a whole hierarchy of powers.

Almost everything that has been said of the spirituality of imperial authority could be repeated here with reference to the pope. He too was a "Christ", the figure who recapitulated the whole body entrusted to him; he led the battle against the forces of darkness in the name of "justice and peace". (These are the two most typical expressions of Gregory VII, who lived in a perpetual conflict.) Terms which denoted the relations between suzerains and vassals, such as "fidelity" and "homage", defined the relations of the faithful to the pope. This is not to say that this meant a secularization of the papacy—that would be to forget the predominantly sacred character of the imperial figure who was the keystone of the feudal structure. It was merely a clericalization of the sacredness which surrounded power. Nevertheless, in passing from the emperor to the pope, the spirituality of authority acquired new emphases. We will conclude this article by considering three of these.

1. Papal authority was built up in a context of struggle, and in this struggle Humbert de Moyenmoutier, Gregory VII and their supporters were fond of maintaining that they were the champions of freedom. The word is astonishing on the lips of such firm defenders of authoritarianism. As used by them, freedom had a variety of meanings, as well as an emotive force going beyond immediate issues. Primarily, it involved in the first place re-establishing the freedom of episcopal and abbatial elections, of maintaining free communications between Rome and local clergies and of removing prelates from too close a dependence on feudal lords. In the second place, it could refer to the liberties of the Italian cities, the allies of the Holy See against Henry IV under Alexander II and later against Barbarossa under Alexander III. But the word "freedom" also suggested a more mystical reality, the "heavenly Jerusalem" of the children of the promise in Gal. 4. 30, which was quoted by St Anselm, whose links with Urban II are well known. In this sense, "freedom" was the power of every Christian to work out his salvation according to his conscience, if need be, in opposition to the State. In the theological outlook of the time, which thought it knew very well what conscience dictated, the ideal of freedom was the decision to live for God in a perspective of communion.[10]

It will be seen here that the pope was regarded as the one who had the true secret of the freedom of the Church and of Christians. This may be felt to be a very dangerous ideology for the freedom of individuals.

2. If the authority of the pope brought freedom, this meant, in the early medieval view, that it guaranteed the domination of the spiritual over the temporal, of the soul over the body. This distinction existed in imperial ideology, but was not treated as an opposition or a strict hierarchy. On the other hand, a sharp insistence on the primacy of the spiritual, identified with the

[10] Cf. Tellenbach, *Libertas, Kirche und Weltordnung* (*Forschung zur Kirchen- und Geistesgeschichte*, VII (Stuttgart, 1936); for the papal theocracy see Pascaut, *La théocratie* (Paris, 1957), Congar, *L'Eglise de s. Augustin à l'époque moderne* (Paris, 1970); Foreville, "Naissance d'une conscience politique dans l'Angleterre du XIIe siècle", in *Entretiens sur la renaissance du 12e siècle*, ed. de Gandillac (Paris, 1968).

authority of the pope, was the favourite theme of the "Gregorian" reformers (the predecessors or partisans of Gregory VII). Cardinal Humbert in 1059 put it like this: "If we wish to make a true and relevant comparison between the dignity of the priesthood and the dignity of kingship, we may say that the priesthood is like the soul and kingship like the body because they love each other mutually, because they need each other and each requires the support of the other. But just as the soul dominates the body and rules over it, the priestly dignity is higher than the royal dignity as heaven is higher than earth. For everything to be in order, the priesthood, like the soul, must decide what should be done and then the kingship, like the head, must give orders to all the members and organize them as necessary. Thus kings must follow churchmen. . . ."[11] In more critical days Gregory VII was to treat the supporters of the empire not merely as the soul treats the body, but as it would treat a rebel body which had become its enemy. In his letter to Hermann of Metz the pope contrasts his own "dignity", with its heavenly origin and direction towards the life above, with that of the king, invented by "human pride" for empty show, "lead" against "gold".[12]

Papal authority became spiritual by repressing the pride of the flesh in the interest of humility and recalling man's heavenly destiny in contrast to a concern with earthly affairs. And yet this authority which challenged the world gradually acquired more power over that world and was itself drawn into earthly and political concerns. The Church's victory in the argument over investiture, instead of freeing the clergy from the grip of feudal institutions, gave them a more comfortable position within them. We are conscious of the paradox that this struggle for the spiritual ended by giving so many temporal powers and tasks to the spiritual men.

We should not think that the men of the twelfth century, after the triumph of the Church in 1122, were insensitive to what shocks us today. They may have been unable to resolve the con-

[11] Cf. *Adversus simoniacos, PL*, CXLIII, col. 1175; French translation in Fliche, *Réforme grégorienne*, I, *op. cit.*, p. 304.
[12] Cf. *PL*, CXLVII, col. 455; translated in Fliche, II, *op. cit.*, p. 312. The extreme depreciation of the civil power in this passage is a recurrent theme of the pope's.

tradition, but they saw its elements. The institutional Church had to face a number of spiritual opposition movements which were (already) denouncing the evils of power and riches in clerical society. St Bernard, for example, scandalized by the growing worldliness of those whose task it was to lead the spiritual struggle, wanted to restore authority to its role of service. Bernard none the less was one of the firmest supporters of the theory of the universal rule of the priesthood (with the image of the "two swords", one in the hand of the prelate, the other wielded at his behest by the hand of the prince). Was it possible that such an authority should, as Bernard would have wished, look no further than the spiritual sphere, that it should prove itself to be wholly at the service of humility and communion among men? The historian must bear in mind both Bernard's utopianism and his disappointment at a Church weighed down by its victories.

3. The struggles of the priesthood and the empire led to a conception of authority as operating at different hierarchical levels, with each authority being something like an emanation of another. In the twelfth century this point of view reinforced the mystique of obedience which introduced those who submitted to it into a line of force which derived ultimately from the divine will. The spirituality of the return to unity, as interpreted by Denys (a return through respect for and contemplation of the successive emanations of the One in the Many), justified and sacralized a whole authoritarian system, in which God was seen through the rule of the Son and the Son through the orders of the earthly hierarchy.

It was especially Hugh of St Victor († 1141) who linked Denys's mysticism with the practical problems of governing the Church and society.[13] Though it led to the contradictions that we have denounced, this whole sacramental and spiritual conception of papal authority was lived by the defenders of the eleventh-century theocracy with evident sincerity in the midst of trials and contradictions. These trials helped to establish the features of the priestly Christ who had to go through suffering to reach his glory. Gregory VII dying abandoned in 1085 was more useful to the cause of the Holy See than the victories of Urban II.

[13] Cf. *Comm. in Hier. coelestem s. Dionysii et de sacramentis christ. fidei*, II, *PL*, CLXXV, col. 130.

III. Conclusion

It has often been said that Christendom has long regarded itself as a huge abbey, and that this explains the importance in this period of the ideas of obedience and authority. This is true. Monks are at the root of the religious exaltation of the emperor and later of the pope. Authority was felt as both a way of contemplating God through his images (or, better, his icons) and also of taking part in the battles of the City of God. In this view the emperor was for a long time equal to the pope, before being violently contrasted with him. The possessor of authority was, in some sense or other, a "cleric", a guide to contemplation and spiritual warfare. A sacrament and a "Christ" of God, he was also a recapitulative figure in whom the community was represented. This last aspect also applied to the monastic order—the superior was elected by his monks and spoke in the name of his house. Cluny, with its federation of almost two thousand monasteries or priories in the twelfth century, is a model of government which might inspire any politician—all the more when we remember the time, in the tenth century, when the empire had ceased to exist and the pope was someone to hide rather than display. The abbots of Cluny, however, travelled all over Christendom. It was a paradoxical constitution since, according to Peter the Venerable, its aim was to eliminate all human and ecclesiastical grandeur. Who will put this constitution into practice?

Translated by Francis McDonagh

Jean Guichard

Ideologies and Power

WE CANNOT speak of power as an object outside ourself. The very way we have to speak is determined by the language of power, depending upon our position in power relationships, whether dominated or dominating others. Thus a reflection on power is always political, in that it can be conducted only from within a social practice tending to fortify or call into question a particular form of power or balance of power.

From this point of view, it may be asked what is the purpose of an examination of power in a theological review. For theological reflection about power has taken place within a church which historically has exercised a form of power, and still does so; a church which for years has dealt with the political powers, and sometimes still does so, each speaking from a position of strength. This means that not even theology begins its discussion of power in all innocence—this discussion takes place too from within a power relationship.

Logic would require, then, that theological reflection should begin by looking at its own ideology of power. What conceptions of power has tradition handed down to us? What part has been played in this tradition by the historical reinterpretation of the practice of Christ towards power, what by the needs of the Church as an institution to survive and develop and what by the establishment of a certain kind of power within the institution itself? What determines the choice by theologians of a particular political reference in their exposition of power? Here we have a very concrete starting-point for a reflection on the theme of power and ideology.

I. DIFFICULTIES OF CHRISTIAN THOUGHT WITH REGARD TO POWER

Note, for example, that since Christianity has ceased to be the main vehicle of the dominant moral and social values, and since the Church has been deprived of the "power" symbolized by the possession of a temporal state, it seems to have had some difficulty in grasping the reality of the new powers established in early Christianity. It is as though the Church, accustomed to anointing kings and thinking of itself as a "perfect society" and the obligatory reference point of all other powers, bestowed by God through his intermediary, were still thinking of the "temporal" powers according to its image of itself. Thus just as in the Church power is thought of as "responsibility for service in the community",[1] so political power is always thought of by the Church in terms of service, common good and the general interest. And just as in the Church the "mandate" of God, the basis of the authority and obligation to serve of the hierarchy, "possesses the functional character of social superiority",[2] to which the community must submit, so political power must be respected by the people, as of divine origin. Respect for the established powers—apart from the case of obvious tyranny—remains a constant in the thought of the Church.

We shall not discuss the question whether in fact the Church's image of itself has not historically been very dependent upon particular philosophical and political models. We shall turn instead to another question. Has the dominant ideology of power in the Church not concealed the reality of power relationships? It certainly seems possible to identify two aspects of this misunderstanding.

(a) On the one hand Christian thought seems to find it difficult to grasp the unity and mutual relationship of the various political, economic and ideological powers. It usually draws upon theories which emphasize the multiplicity of powers rather than

[1] Paul VI: Audience at the Tribunal of the Sacred Roman Rota (*Osservatore Romano*, 29 Jan. 1971).
[2] *Ibid.* For the Christian conception of political power, cf., for example, *Octogesima Adveniens*, No. 46.

their unity. This inability to think in a unified fashion is found at every level. It was visible in the structure of the Constitution *Gaudium et spes*. It is found in most encyclicals which deal with economic power, and do not place it in an organic relationship to political power. In a business,[3] a distinction is made between "economic power" (the "external" conditions for the work of the business) and "technical power" (the internal organization of the enterprise) without establishing any clear relationship between the objective constraint of the first and the great freedom which seems to be left to the manager of the business—unity of management being declared indispensable—to make the factory a community of persons all called to participate and not merely to carry out orders. A text such as this seems to overlook the intimate relationship between a form of economic organization and a pattern of hierarchy and power within the business. The unity of a society is found elsewhere than within itself.

(b) This leads to the conclusion that theology has overlooked the basis of power relationships in capitalist societies. This basis has been the main interest of Marxist analysis. It is by virtue of the act of selling his labour for a wage that the proletarian (one who possesses only his labour and is forced to sell it) becomes dependent upon him who owns the tools of his work. Thus the power which capital exercises over labour does not derive from a political or ideological constraint external or prior to the act of work, but from the very act of selling his labour, which the workeɩ is forced to carry out in order to live. More precisely, then, a proletarian is subject not to another man, but to the means of production themselves, to capital, of which the capitalist himself is only an agent. Every personal power relationship is abolished and replaced by the power of personified objects, reified persons.[4]

II. Power Relationships are inherent in the Social Structure

Power relationships, then, are not inter-personal phenomena. The relationships of domination and subordination lie beyond the

[3] Cf. Paul VI, Allocution to the Centre Chrétien des patrons et dirigeants d'entreprise française, DC, 26 April 1972 (French text, O.R., 23 March 1972).

[4] Cf. particularly Marx, *Un chapitre inédit du Capital*, 10/18, 1971, pp. 249–50.

goodwill of the individual and are inherent in the objective place occupied by individuals in production relationships. The situation of groups of men—social classes—with relation to others, in positions of domination or subordination, is a function of their place in the production relationship. Thus as the law makes clear, the wage earner is defined by his state of dependence upon his employer; and in the French legal code the hiring of his labour is treated under the same heading as the hiring of objects or animals. This is reflected in a joke which is often heard amongst young French peasants: "I lent you my boar to serve your sow, lend me your son to plough my field."

It is only too obvious that these objective hierarchical relationships are coupled in individuals with a personal awareness of their social superiority or inferiority. From early childhood, an awareness of social hierarchy is embedded in the psychology of individuals. The children of different social classes do not live in the same parts of town, share neither their play, nor, as far as possible, their studies; and later, if they come together in sexual activity, this is usually regarded as abnormal or even criminal when the sense of class hierarchy is linked to that of racial hierarchy, as in the case of the negroes in the U.S.A. or immigrant workers in places such as France or Switzerland. Thus from infancy any breach of the hierarchy is regarded as an act contrary to the natural order of things, which society must repress.

We shall return to the importance of this psychological and moral internalization of the power relationships inherent in the social order. But it is first necessary to emphasize the existence of these structural relationships of domination and subordination, for if they are forgotten, it is possible to give the impression that these moral and psychological phenomena exist on their own account, that they are the product of personal wickedness, inherent in the heart of man, and that therefore they can be corrected solely by the inner conversion of the individual.

III. Religious Ideology and Power

It is in this way that religious ideology, emphasizing in this discussion of power the phenomena of personal service, serves to hide from people the reality of the oppression and exploitation undergone by those classes which are dependent and subordinate. In the text quoted above,[5] Paul VI says, for example, to Christian employers: "You must first of all pay attention to the concrete attitude of persons, to what is revealed by their behaviour in the face of power and the growing demands of responsibility, and this should lead to a genuine renewal of life which as far as possible takes in the real mentality of employers and managers, with its values, its riches and its limits. Thus any adjustment or change in structures will be rooted in an openness and a conversion of the heart which will avoid the fearful blockages from which our society suffers."

Traditional Christian ideology continues basically to argue in the same way as Leo XIII did in his encyclicals at the end of the last century—there are social classes and inequalities, but this is inevitable and in accordance with nature and the will of God. The social injustices which result from this can be remedied by fraternal co-operation between classes, by defining a moral code, reciprocal rights and duties between employers and workers, and so forth, "without prejudice to property and persons", in the words of an expression which oddly enough is found in the writings both of the bourgeois legislators in a tradition of the rights of man and of Christian thinkers for a century. Thus the requirement of charity—formulated in terms of the recognition of personal dignity outside any social structure—reinforces and sanctions with the seal of religion the social relationships in which injustice and oppression are structurally inherent.

But this is the role of the dominant ideology of our societies, to conceal structural power relationships behind the appearance of personal equality. The work contract, although it establishes a dependence relationship, is still presented as a free contract between the possessors of goods (labour in one case and means of production in another), who are free and equal individuals in law (the wage is presented as the equivalent of the labour) and the subordinated classes cease to be aware of the mechanisms of exploitation in power. At every other level of social existence, the same legal equality and liberty of individual persons are proclaimed: political equality in the vote (employer and worker have

[5] Cf. note 3.

only one vote each), in taxation, in schooling, etc. This ideological camouflage must be torn away to reveal this fiction of liberty, this profound inequality inherent in the social structures and concealed by the forms of law and the State. It is always even more difficult to destroy this camouflage if it is sanctioned by religion. It is not surprising that, in the nineteenth century, the battle against capitalist power was never separated from the struggle against religious ideology.

IV. POLITICAL POWER AND IDEOLOGICAL CONSENSUS

One may say that the power relationships inherent in the very structure of society are reflected at every level of any particular society, particularly in terms of political power and ideology, through which the social structure becomes part of the psychology of individuals.

1. *Political power.* Liberal analysis, like Marxist analysis, though in different terms, has always considered political power as a necessary guarantee, as the key-stone of the social relationships established in the organization of economic production. In this sense, behind a relative autonomy and an apparent diversity, there is a real unity of power. The function of the State as policeman or night-watchman is to bring about a respect for order in a society in which, according to the liberal analysis, nature has endowed certain individuals with ownership and called them to govern the mass of inferior individuals who are not owners.[6] The State, according to Marx, is always the State of the ruling class; all power is class power.

The very existence of any power reflects the existence of domination relationships within society. State power is only justified in relation to a society divided into antagonistic classes. This is why Marxist tradition has always linked the establishment of a

---

[6] André Vachet, *L'Idéologie libérale, L'individu et sa propriété* (Paris, 1970). For the Marxist conception of power cf. Nikos Poulantzas, *Pouvoir Politique et classes sociales* (Paris, 1971); see the important methodological comments in Maxime Rodinson, *Marxisme et monde musulman* (Paris, 1972), particularly Part II: "Luttes nationales et luttes de classes"; Anouar Abdel-Malek, *La dialectique sociale* (Paris, 1972), IV: "Sociologie du pouvoir"; Barrington Moore, *Social Origins of Dictatorship and Democracy* (Boston, 1967).

classless society with the withering away of the State, the disappearance of political power.

Thus the State has a repressive role, that of imposing upon the subordinate classes, by force and by law, the acceptance of social relationships which oppress them.

2. *Ideological consensus.* But no power can maintain itself for long by the use of violence alone—power needs a popular consensus, a spontaneous acceptance of the existing domination relationships, and internal recognition that one's own subordination is necessary to social life in conformity with transcendent moral (and sometimes religious) values and aimed at assuring the happiness of everyone.

This is increasingly necessary, in the first instance, in any business, a fact that has been understood by employers for several years.[7] Participation, workers' shareholding, joint planning, the politics of productivity deals and so forth are all intended to give the subject classes a material and psychological interest in the existing social relationships within the business. The mental structures of the wage earners have got to be such as enable them to accept psychologically the new demands of capitalist growth.

But this process of integration of the subordinate classes is reproduced at every level of social life under the increasingly direct control of the State. In the capitalism of growth and consumption the problem of the reproduction and internalization of production relationships is becoming increasingly central.[8] This

[7] Cf., for example, the text of the *Conseil du progrès industriel* recommending that the commitment of the staff to the purposes of the business, particularly with the aid of a house journal: "This journal must not hesitate to welcome editors who would undertake a real education of the readers concerning the role of the firm in the creation and distribution of prosperity, and will explain the fundamental ideas which are the basis and justification of industrial civilization. This is a real philosophy, with which all the staff must be imbued so that the whole business aims at becoming more competitive. To this end, the idea of profit in the system of competition must be forcefully rehabilitated as the tangible sign and measure of the creation of prosperity and of the value of the individuals who obtain it." Quoted by Pierre Ranval, *Hiérarchie des salaires et luttes des classes* (Paris, 1972), p. 49. See also Michel Drancourt, "Pour une nouvelle théorie du pouvoir", in *Réalités*, 156 (1959), pp. 25-9.

[8] As we cannot take this theme further here, we draw attention in particular to the work by Henri Lefebvre, "La réproduction des rapports de production", *L'Homme et la Société*, Nos. 22 and 23 (Oct. 1971–Jan. 1972).

is the point at which pressure is exercised by a certain number of institutions—the family, the army, the school, information and culture—which makes certain amongst the mass of the people of the material and ideological reproduction of the conditions of production, the diffusion of moral and social values which correspond to the requirements of the social organization for its functioning. Ideological practice is a form and a necessary condition for economic and political power.

There is a direct link between the retention of power and the control of the places in which ideology is worked out and transmitted. That is why such places are increasingly the object of revolutionary struggle.[9] Ideological struggle is a necessary dimension of every battle against the existing powers.

To the extent in which the Church still plays an important role in the ideological confirmation of power, it too becomes the place and the prize of any struggle for the radical transformation of the world.[10]

Translated by R. A. Wilson

[9] Cf. Louis Althusser, "Idéologie et Appareils Idéologiques d'Etat", *La Pensée*, 151 (June 1970), pp. 3–38. On the school, see the excellent documentation provided by *Lettre* (68, *rue de Babylone*, Paris 7°), Nos. 169–170 (Sept., Oct. 1972). For the whole group of ideological problems, the work of Antonio Gramsci, *Opere,* 13 volumes (Turin), remains essential. There is a bibliography in the remarkable work by Hughes Portelli, *Gramsci et le bloc historique* (Paris, 1972).

[10] Cf., for example, "Document final de la rencontre latino-américaine 'Chrétiens pour le socialisme' " (*Lettre*, No. 166, June 1972); and the special number of *Lettre*, No. 173, "Les chrétiens et la politique."

Hermann Josef Wallraff

Interest Groups and Power

IT IS now just over a hundred years since the authorities graciously granted their subjects the right to combine in organizations. The right was only reluctantly and hesitantly recognized. Many Cassandras bewailed the step. Even liberals expressed concern; their worry was about the freedom of the individual which had been only with great effort secured from the constricting network of companies, guilds and concessions.

Those in civil authority saw in any union or association, whatever form it took, the first step to a new conspiracy. The rulers were confident in their ability to remain master of the individual citizens, but movements and above all unions and extra-local associations were in their eyes the first signs of new disturbances. The authorities assumed that to give the citizens the right of association would sooner or later add further unhappy dates to the list of the revolutionary years 1789, 1830 and 1848.

The parallel liberal horror of unions of employees was felt mainly by the better off. All those whose income, property, or political rights raised them above the average for the population had no trouble in paying homage to individualism. Compared with individual employees, they could take a much more relaxed attitude, in so far as it was a matter of helping themselves. It was hardly surprising that in these circles people had little time for interest groups.

Most people had to depend on unions for the defence of their interests and they were consequently acutely aware of the value of such groupings. They had to overcome the efforts firstly of the co🗝ervative aristocrats and rulers and secondly of the established economic order to prevent the formation of unions and associations. Their unity, however, gradually enabled them to hold their own against their strong bargaining partners. Through their representation in trade unions and similar bodies, they gradually became able to exert influence on the holders of national and local authority in the pre-political sphere, as the democratic franchise had previously enabled them to do in the political sphere.

It soon became clear that the importance of interest groups was not limited to the expression of the material interests and other aims of their members. They also brought important benefits to the community as a whole. For example, they divided the community into a complex and very flexible network of representative bodies. By this means they prevented the isolation of individual citizens among so many others, and curbed their feeling of standing alone against a state in which power was inaccessible. Within the State there were local authorities and local associations, but even at this level procedures were official. They may have been closer to the individual citizens than a unitary or even a federal state, but the need for solidarity, which is strong in most people, is not met by mere identification with the official structures of the local community.

Large and complex industrial societies are so difficult for their individual members to comprehend that, left to himself, the individual finds it hard to say at what point of the whole he lives and acts. Individuals in such systems do not really know how they should behave, or what they may or may not expect. It was interest groups which first succeeded in giving the average citizen the feeling that he now knew at least something about his social environment. Free interest groups also bring together the thousands and thousands of individual opinions and intentions. Being forced to speak with a single voice, they inevitably smooth down extreme aims and demands. In other words, by private action these free organizations make their members capable of forming united demands. They also put social groups in a position to make agreements with each other as groups. By increasing the range of their members, they increase the range of private forces as a whole.

Among the most important of the advantages of the existence and activity of interest groups is the fact that many of them work for the vast majority of the population. Because of their expert staffs, they generally see more quickly than the population as a whole the important socio-economic developments. They publicize the relevant factors at a relatively early stage, and do so in such a way that it is possible for ordinary citizens to assimilate immediately necessary information. In the meetings organized by these associations, the participants come from the same professional or trade branch, which means that they have a common language. Everyone knows more or less what is going on. Many people who are eager to take an active part in shaping society are in this way enabled to do so in areas with which they are relatively familiar. By making this possible, private groupings contribute to giving scope to ideas of autonomy, and thereby widen the sphere of freedom. From a technical point of view, the State or local authorities could carry out most of the tasks which are usually regarded as most important in stimulating the formation of interest groups. But then in practice the State would become an all-powerful, frightening authority. An opportunity to divide the powers necessary for public life would also be wasted, which, if things went wrong, would be detrimental to civil rights, not least the rights of those citizens who, individually, are anything but powerful.

No serious observer would expect private associations and groupings, alone among historical organizations, to be without problems. One problem is that some sectors of society are not represented by interest groups while others can make use of powerful groupings. This difference is all the more important because associations can influence the decisions which affect the distribution of the social product. It can come about that social forces which originated in a desire to alter a distorted distribution of the social product by those in power in their turn get into a position which enables them to dominate groups which changed circumstances have forced into a weaker position. In the case of one set of these stronger groups, the trade unions in the important sectors of the national economy, the superiority which they enjoy in relation to the unorganized or weakly organized sectors of the population is to some extent counterbalanced by the fact that in the meantime the employers with whom they deal have combined to form influential organizations. The employers and property-owners long ago grew out of their original attachment to individualism. Generally strong interest groups are balanced by equally strong opposing groups. This is only true, however, as long as the interests of the unions, for example, conflict with those of the employers. If, however, they have common aims, which is not unusual, the power of the one group reinforces that of the other. Both sides join forces against third parties, which, lacking this double power, are generally weaker. This is where the problems begin.

An even more difficult problem is the fact that large or strategically placed interest groups, organizations operating in parallel and the extensive network of interest groups which develop from these may succeed in their aims, openly or secretly, at the expense of the common good. They are experienced in putting forward their private demands with appeals to the common good, and indeed are never at a loss for appropriate phrases. Organizations enjoying economic importance also come to see themselves as businesses, in that they too feel justified in pursuing their aims without restriction so long as there are no explicit laws against this. Perhaps not officially, but no less definitely, to judge from their actions, the interest groups have taken over the idea of harmony accepted by the early industrial firms. In the midst of fierce competition, they believed that an "invisible hand" operated to direct their various energetic pursuits of profit to the common good. Apart from the blind spots which this optimism had from its beginning, it has become clear that it was only tenable in liberal economic theory as long as that theory did not have to bother about monopolies and close-knit oligopolies. To defend it in the face of all the powerful decision-making centres which have come into economic life with the interest groups can be little more than an ironic joke. No sufficiently reliable way has yet been discovered to link the thick tangle of interest groups which are inevitably of very great importance for the further development of the community as a whole and the State in particular with the plans which are intended to take the community forward into the future. The

likely contribution of a revived concept of harmony to this problem is even more disappointing than that of its original version.

Powerful interest groups do not automatically counterbalance
each other. A balance must therefore be deliberately constructed.
In Western Germany this idea led to an attempt to bring the
most important organizations into joint discussions. Representatives of the Federal Government, the state governments and the
cities would meet round the same table. At this "table of reason"
the representatives of the public and the representatives of private
interests would exchange views on the status and future of the
community, inform each other of their plans and decide jointly
on their actions to avoid any damage to the common good. It is
hoped that this will, for example, prevent the sum of claims from
exceeding the total of the social product and undermining the
stability of the currency. The aim is to achieve concerted action,
an orchestra of the powerful, a chorus in which no single voice
drowns the rest.

So far the gap between the idea of concerted action and its implementation has been wide. It was remarkable that quite early
on, when the number of participants in the discussion had been
kept to what was felt to be manageable, urgent requests were
made by other interested parties that they should be brought in
too. Such assiduity is not generally apparent when contributions
have to be made or restrictions accepted, and from the behaviour
of the participants it looks as though concerted action is little
more than a means by which powerful interests seek to advance
themselves.

Many observers believe that the reason for the failure of concerted action to restrain private organizations from making un-
fair use of their power is that the proceedings at the "table of
reason" deliberately do not go beyond dialogue, and no binding
decisions are made. For this reason these critics suggest that concerted action should be replaced by an official economic and
social council. This would be an organ of government, like a
third chamber of deputies, in which, as at present, interested
parties would be represented, but it would also have power to
take decisions. The decisions taken would then have to be carried out by even the most powerful of the interest groups. In

view of previous experience of such institutions in other countries, however, it would be unwise to expect too much from such an organ. The main reason is that the powers whose activity is to be limited must themselves contribute to that limitation, and they do this, if at all, only with the greatest reluctance.

The same criticism may be made of the proposal that the state authorities should introduce special laws to prevent interest groups from pursuing their private ends at the expense of the community. It is suggested that these strong groupings should be placed under special supervision. Conservative circles immediately think in this context of one or other form of trade union law, which is a revealing example of how difficult objective judgments are in this field. It is generally an interest which opposes another interest group, even when the action is taken under the auspices of the State. Social groups which are accustomed to make use of the state machinery for their own purposes immediately protest when the process is reversed and the restrictions affect them. No wonder this attitude spreads, with the result that the State finds it difficult to oppose the positions of power which exist in the private sphere. On the level of interest groups it is likely to have no more success than the very modest amount it has had in its dealings with cartels and combines.

What, then, are the real possibilities? Above all, public opinion must preserve a constructive and critical distance. The public must remain sympathetic to private organizations, because otherwise the important values which depend on the existence and activity of these groups for their implementation would be endangered. It must be all the more critical since it can be a most effective counter-force. If a group puts forward a demand which wins no support among the public, the demand will be hard to meet. In practice, "public opinion" here refers in particular to all the forces and positions which can exercise any degree of influence on the public, the press, radio and television commentators, the spokesman for a theoretically based economic policy and representatives of institutions whose judgments are normally based on ethics rather than material interests. Unfortunately experience shows that these and other social forces tend to act, consciously or unconsciously, as lobbies. Thus the task of preventing the power which has developed among interest groups from having destructive effects turns out to mean developing the faculty of independent critical judgment and giving it a certain latitude in which to operate. That this is precisely the task which has always presented itself when dealing with power is not surprising. The danger is more in power and its extent than in the people who possess it.

Translated by Francis McDonagh

Candido Mendes de Almeida

The Exercise of Power in Developing Countries

IN THIS essay I put forward the Brazilian example as typical of the full maturation of a national development process resulting from an economy directed towards the outside market, and from specialization in the supply of so-called colonial products. Of course there is no reason why conclusions relating to Brazil should not apply to analogous situations in the same hemisphere and with a similar setting. Hence my use of the term "Latin America" in the present context.

An examination of the question of power today in an international perspective but in regard to the developing countries and the foregoing delimitation requires an analysis of three distinct phases.

1. The first, which in Latin America continued practically without any change right up to the nineteen-thirties, was that of the full integration of these countries into the *international* system of the division of labour, in which they functioned mainly as exporters of raw materials and importers of manufactured goods. This period gave rise to a general form of government (usually known as the "colonial structure") which has come to be characteristic, in the standard dysfunctions of its economic, political and social behaviour, of the typical panorama of underdevelopment.

2. The second phase featured a dominant *national* characteristic and emphasized emerging internal markets. It showed an attempt to move beyond the colonial structure by means of a

vigorous aid programme in the public sector. This was the so-called period of spontaneous development, which extended from the post-war period of 1945 almost until the mid-nineteen-sixties.

3. Thereafter began the third phase, and, with the end of the process of import substitution, a crisis in the former spontaneity, taking the form (within the change process) of a major increase in inflation and a recession in GNP growth. This stage was and is marked by attempts to rationalize development under the rule of authoritarian technocracies. The intention is to reconcile agile public planning with the new influx of external capital and the development of a pact strategy between major public enterprise and the multinational companies.

It is important to explain how power is articulated in these various structures and to what extent it is effectively controlled by the national State in this process of development which, historically, has formed a "boomerang" curve, departing from external domination (for the present) with the end of the phase of spontaneity, in order to recover a place in the international system as a decisive variable component of its dynamic thrust.

In each of these phases there is a variation either of the individualization of the political infrasystem as a decision centre, or the position of the State as the main protagonist in the process.

I. Colonial Export Regime and the Dominance of Economics over Politics

In these terms, for example, there was in the first period a clear absence of any "substantivization" of the political phenomenon as affected by the formations of the economic infrasystem, such as those dynamic processes and demands imposed on it in its international and global setting. In this sense the action of the State was wholly that of a superstructure implied and operated by the system in order to maintain the general inertia inherent in the system.

There is no reason to speak of a "substantive" state intervention in the process; the thrust of the regime was directed not towards change or crisis, but towards the permanent conservation of its "homeostasis".

The functions of power, all subserving the demands of the

system, are characteristic of specific politics and actions. But these cannot be considered as autonomous causality vectors but as corollaries and sequels of the perfect functioning of a regime in which the national territory features as an exporter of raw materials in the overall process of the division of labour.

In such a framework, it would be appropriate to power to correct, by local absorption, any retractions of the international surplus circulation of a specific product; to siphon off, on the basis of relative internal redistributions, the excess manpower available in such production sectors; to ensure compatibility between the rural complex and the system's inchoate fundamental service requirements. Such a framework will offer, for example, as specific products, oligarchic and consumer policies which are to all intents and purposes part and parcel of such a system.

II. DEVELOPMENT AND AUTONOMIZATION OF POWER AND POLITICAL ACTION

Hence the take-off phase of development is identical with that stage in which the political element of the process takes over the direction. It was not only by a deliberate and forceful intervention in this inertia that an attempt was made to overcome the crisis of the nineteen-thirties, but in a radical assumption of such action by the State. This cannot be described as a superstructure of groups or classes sufficiently mature to be able to transfer their programme into the field of organized power. Direct state action precedes this formation to the very extent that the regime and its involutive differentiation did not allow the free play of classes and their dynamic movement in the history of these *collectivities*.

Hence a state apparatus precedes the effective emergencee of a society, just as in the colonial regime there is no development of the function of enterprise or of any of the mechanisms of mediation for those interests in which the social process begins to take effect.

Therefore it was no sovereign arbiter State with complex and necessarily contradictory aspirations which emerged towards the mid-century in Latin American countries, but a political power promoting, *per se*, a new social order and a break with the previous structure. Its autonomy came to occupy the space vacated because of the fractures and retractions then obvious in the international system. However, the actions of its occasional representatives caused an authentic and increasing articulation with a functional society. Hence it accorded with an internal industrial bourgeoisie in the course of formation, with an urban proletariat and the new technical settings in which the professional middle class operated. But a State with a nationalist vocation controlled the process. For the first time its politics took the opposite direction to that represented by the rules of the game as obeyed by the colonial structure and its new secular version.

III. THE ACTUAL POWERS OF NATIONAL DEVELOPMENT

The state power in such a process first of all depends on direct intervention in the production process; acting as entrepreneur in the setting up of basic industries and of the infrastructure called for by the accelerated development of an industrialization programme, with an autarchic dominant characteristic in the present case, and wholly directed towards the creation and dynamization of its own internal market. In addition to these tasks there are the powers of control and redevelopment of the national income and its manipulation. This is shown primarily in the decisions on the establishment of a minimum salary in a country like Brazil, requiring for the first time the constitution of an internal market of general-order consumer goods.

Such powers would be supplemented by intersector revenue transfers: what has been called *"confisco cambial"*, the aim of which was to bring about an economizing in traditional sectors always linked to the export economy, in the direction of an industrial expansion intended to produce an integrated reserve and an effectively self-sustained expansion process. Hence it was a primarily national "intermezzo" oriented towards internal markets which, in Brazil, was characteristic of the immediate postwar period and enabled that stage to be extended to the end of the nineteen-fifties; there then evolved the ideology of development controlled by its internal expansion threshold, and capable of allowing (by reason of the multipl' .ity of local initiatives) a relative levelling of world prosperit' imbalances.

Those phenomena are well known which led to the collapse of the phase of the populist and national expansion of the former peripheries of the colonial regime.

We have to take into account the contamination between the external and internal price increases which characterized the effort of underdeveloped nations for a maximum valorization of the results of their traditional export economy, in order to make sure of their internal growth before any impact was felt of the continuous action of the deterioration of exchange terms on the international market. The State resorted to the rash expedient of open inflation to try to complete the industrialization process. Even though it found the material means to do that, it simultaneously destroyed the monetary dimension of the economy. When inflation reached a rate of 106 per cent in Brazil, not only the chance of internal economies in the country was wiped out: the State lost its effective capacity to direct the redistribution of revenue characteristic of its effective power during the nineteen-forties and fifties. It replaced that by an alternate and automatic series of nominal actions without even the public capacity to direct the process or to impose a specific model on it. A statism which was both gigantic and inactive emerged from this phase, corresponding to the deep social erosion of differentiated groups and interests in the process which it had started, and in the course of which the internal industrial bourgeoisie disappeared too. The entire dynamism of the third phase of the process was to depend on the capacity of the vast public apparatus (created and emasculated during the previous phase) to oppose and control new rationalized trends in foreign capital and in the new system of internal relations which was to prove characteristic of the present decade.

IV. THE STATE AND THE SUPER-ENTERPRISE OF THE SEVENTIES

The present stage in the increase of power relations in the underdeveloped countries is characterized from the internal viewpoint by the balance of assets at the disposal of the State and big business for obtaining ultimate control of that rationalized development model which replaced the spontaneity of the nineteen-fifties. There is no need to insist on the great difference between the framework of the nineteen-seventies from that of the period of twenty years ago which produced the perspectives of a *Populorum Progressio* or an "Alliance for Progress".

For those countries which progressed most in the nineteen-fifties, such as Brazil or Argentina, the so-called import substitution process is now at an end. They have reached the point of establishing all the industrial equipment on their own territory. After stretching the monetary dimension of their economy for that purpose, they can (not without difficulty but decisively) reconstitute it by an entirely new policy of control and reorientation of national revenue. That is also the task of authoritarian planning regimes which have replaced the former populism. Their effort is to ensure the controlled implementation of the vast machinery of economic intervention which they have retained; and to start at the same time a drastic formation of internal economies, with the risk of an economic concentration and a compartmentalization of the revitalizing process. This latter effort is implemented within a new framework of international conditioning factors wholly different from the former international organization, in a stage of exchange between world centre and periphery on the basis of raw materials exports and manufactured goods imports.

V. The Entry of Big Business into Development

The major priority for international capitalism today is to win possibilities of industrial production in the former colonial countries which were already markets for general consumer goods. Of course there is a calculated risk in coexistence between this public apparatus (drastically reorientated during the populist phase) and an international system on which it relied to beat the initial stagnation period by trusting in an inflow of external resources to recover the transformation rhythm interrupted at the beginning of the nineteen-sixties. Despite the vast facilities granted at the beginning of this phase, recourse to external capital was had in an entirely different way to investment in the "hot money" phase, or the migrations of resources at the beginning of the century.

This new inflow of capital occurred not only in the extremely selective area of interests but also, increasingly, by means of the replacement of actual economic resources by "know how" and "invisible" finance. It also increased its ascendancy over the pre-existing national capital, thanks to the change in the scale economy from spontaneous development, and in the strategies of the super-businesses and multinational companies.

This balance-sheet requires the substitution of the radical perspective of imbalance between the developed and the underdeveloped world, within a framework which has usually given rise to an asymmetrical regime in international relations.

VI. Colonial Dependence and Marginality in International Relations

In the former situation of colonial dependence the two poles of the relation (though in a very imbalanced way) were organically articulated in an exchange relationship within the "colonial pact". Nowadays we are aware of the repertory of control relations characteristic of a hegemonic centre, including the perspective of definitively marginalized peripheries within these complexes. Among these powers there are:

(a) *The formation of artificial export ceilings.* The consumption needs of the affluent countries are divided accordingly among different supply centres—the developing countries—so that all get a share of the trade, but at the price of a permanent *under-employment* of their production capacity. These products have a high storage flexibility, and each producer country is capable of becoming the dominant supplier to the international market. No conference on the present raw materials situation in the world can forget that the producing market has a decisive instrument for discouraging any export price valorization policy that the producing nations might care to apply.

(b) *The forced comparison between non-competitive export prices.* A second typical control technique of contemporary international commerce results from the capacity of the present centres of world economy to influence a very wide exchange field, and to carry out therein transactions in regard to one and the same product obtained at very different cost levels.

In the traditional capitalist-economy regimes the non-compressibility of production costs was the indispensable condition for the specification of a colonial economy. In the asymmetrical situation, however, the provision of an import programme like that of the consumer markets of the affluent economy would be affected more by a concern to discipline the external trade of these countries in imposing a quota system than by the mechanism of selection by minimal prices which export articles could reach. A control of this kind results from the fact that the external-market discipline of an asymmetrical economy, the custodian of the new processing systems of the colonial regimes which trade with it, becomes continually less economical and more political.

(c) *Storage policy.* Another consequence of asymmetry is the tendency to release the volume of international trade from the effective needs of the buying markets. They manifest an increasing storage capacity in which the regime would take refuge in any scarcity situation, mainly through an interruption of supplies in the case of a new world conflict. The market also benefits from a new regulative international price mechanism for these articles, like that representing the effect on the upper market of the possibility of supplying accumulated surpluses to the external trade market.

(d) *The monopoly of technological research and the substitution of synthetic products.* The disparity in economic progress between centre and periphery means (to the profit of the dominant economy) a confirmation of the existing monopoly of the industrial exploitation of new techniques of production, in particular in regard to the replacement of tropical by synthetic products. The buying centres therefore very often retain the capacity to decide the subsistence on the market of some traditional peripheral exports.

VII. BIG BUSINESS AND ITS POWERS

Given such a framework, it is necessary to determine the powers possessed by the State (in the setting of the military technocracies of the continent) and big business, for obtaining ultimate control over the revitalization process, evident today in the underdeveloped nations, and particularly in their more complex and more dynamic processes, as in Brazil.

Big business possesses the following elements of intervention:

(*a*) A demand for economic concentration, featuring the transformation of the scale economy. The change in the economic profile of the new model required above all a large-scale offensive to ensure a massive application of the "know how" and "invisible quanta" to guarantee specific technological models or the "capital-intensive" structure which this experiment postulated. Hence there was an abandonment of any idea of using the abundant growth-equation factors of underdeveloped countries, emphasizing more the speed of the process than the maximization of possibilities actually available at such points in the processes. The strategy applied was one of territory *polarization*, into integrated zones and regions eccentric to its controlled expansion.

(*b*) *The effect upon this expansion of the previous existence of a market reserve in the economic area.* This is dictated by the search for economic inter-complementarities with the aim of reaching the pre-existent monetary-economy zone, and putting into effect a supra-national integration project based on the advantages of the "islands of prosperity" already existing on the continent. This project would be permeated by the philosophy of the Latin-American common market, which appears more as an ideological project for the most dynamic area of the new neo-capitalist model of the hemisphere than as a promotional vision of development, i.e., an interiorization of growth strategies and efforts for direct absorption of subsistency-economy pockets in the marginalized areas of the continent.

VIII. Emergent State Controls

As the Brazilian example indicates, nowadays the State tends to reaffirm its desire to run the process, by calling on the following powers and controls:

(*a*) The use of mechanisms still capable of being put at the service of the formation of public funds deriving from the rationalization of the collection apparatus and the total takeover of the sub-collection system provoked by the inflationist period. In this way, in a short period, a fiscal structure is attained with a profile close to that of the mature economies, with a more marked emphasis on direct taxation and an effective, democratic generalization of income tax.

(*b*) A drastic recourse to new economies including the slowing down of tax redistribution, a restriction of the buying power of most salaries, and an enlargement of incitements directed towards the strategic areas of revitalization policy.

(*c*) Discipline by planning the occupation of the national territory, including the imposition of various regional models for expansion.

(*d*) The imposition of a service economy on the entire public-sector apparatus, in recovering the effective control capacity of the strategic core of the economy (represented by the entire communications network of the country, by half the energy produced, by two-thirds of the iron and steel production, by a monopoly of petrol production, and by substantial sectors of the basic processing industries).

(*e*) Control of the national economy and its conversion towards open liberalization, in the form of a non-discriminatory issue on, for the first time, a wholly free stock market. Such powers are exercised in the rigorous selection of credit for general consumer goods, on the money markets, and above all in investment banks.

By means of the ascendancy won by manipulating these controls, the State has been able, even just within the limits of an ostensible legal statute, to control the size of mergers and the definitions of framework or setting within which international capital could try to establish a hegemony, by defining the overall systemic conditions for its intervention. This kind of control would culminate in the creation of preferential conditions for public enterprises on the share market, in a major manipulation of facilities, and in advantages conceded to open capital.

(*f*) A control of the possibilities of social development apparent above all in health policies, and in urbanization and housing; this control is also applicable as the instrument of an anti-cyclic policy in the depression phases of a market economy.

By means of the whole range of the vast financial apparatus available within this flexible structure for regulating the economic process, there arose an empirical coexistence regime; it became more obvious to the extent that development occurred by virtue of ultimate control by public power in models of this kind. Such a perspective could amount to an intercomplementarity of roles within the unprecedented framework of fusion between multinational enterprises and the public sector, as has been demonstrated in Brazil during the last few years, especially in the area of exploitation of non-ferrous metals and their exportation. This example should show, primarily, the still marginal nature that the new external orientation would give to convergence between governmental interest and that of big business in a global strategy of multinational enterprises. But at the same time it should demonstrate the degree of interdependence and the mediating projects in which present relations between the external and internal sectors of these processes are expressed; above all, the disruptive conditions which affect any violation by national states of the rules which make them universally dependent on the markets; the control which can occur in the production area is to a considerable extent corrected, or compensated, by the hegemony of international commercial or financial control, on which it depends.

IX. CONDEMNATION TO COEXISTENCE

Acute observers will not fail to have noticed the increasing paralysis of nationalization procedures during the last few years, above all when seen on the periphery of financial compensation projects or forms of investment repatriation. With the passing of the "brutal" spontaneity of the nineteen-fifties a point of equilibrium will be reached in the play of advantages and reprisals in the construction of new national development economies; this could constitute a quasi-condemnation to coexistence between the entrepreneur State and the multinational enterprise. It was in these terms, for example, that we witnessed public disapproval of the multinational ITT corporation which in Chile, once again in its former "pattern", found that its intention of opposing the political system and conspiring for its demise was viewed as a marginal act, as piracy. Evidently a new consensus was being formed against the coexistence of these "residual" powers in the underdeveloped countries.

X. The Super-Multinational or a Federation of Public Monopolies?

There is reason to wonder whether the present development will end in the polarization apparent for a decade or so in the confrontation between "Leviathan and Behemoth". A primary possibility will be an eschatological vision of new supranational economies in the hemisphere consolidated in the form of a flexible and decisive superimposition of the area of the super-enterprises. The Latin-American market envisioned would be a "market reserve" guaranteed to the major foreign businesses superimposed on foreign states reduced to the ancillary role of infrastructure suppliers and non-profitable investments necessary for the perfect consolidation of the hegemony of neo-capitalism on the continent.

From the public viewpoint, we might see the counterpart to this vigorous state intervention, recognizing the obsolescence of former territorial limits, and entering a federation of major monopolies in the key-sectors of Latin-American economic development.

XI. Polar and Dialectical Models for Latin America

The most likely outcome is a dialectical rather than a polar result to the confrontation. The future of the continent, with and after the versatility shown at present by the technocracies of the period of transformation, would seem rather to reside in a new diversification of plans, measures and inputs in which we would see a dilution of the former unitary vision of the protagonists in the process. The present success of Brazilian development seems to a large extent dependent on the flexibility with which the public sector has staggered the international contribution and confronted the inputs it accepted with a new complex of conditioning factors; these last have substantially fulfilled its power projects. Foreign business would be seen to some degree as purloining the soil on which it established itself in order to exercise its traditional hegemony, in counterpart (both subtle and elusive) to the present characteristics of the "asymmetrical" system already noted in international trade reports.

With its differentiated character, and operating as it does with a multiple strategy, this possibility had to some extent already been anticipated in the demand for a broad knowledge of all the factors and all the forces at present effective on the international scene, so as to obtain both an exhaustive map of the particular circumstances that are its actual framework, and the inadequate localization differentiated between factors and actors applicable national enterprises.

From this angle it is surely possible, despite all one's cavils, to get the most fruitful results from UNCTAD III: significantly these points also occurred in the proposals of the Vatican delegation at that conference. The following were the demands made:

(*a*) Recognition of the entire framework of protagonists in the international domain for example by imposing a law and rules of operation on multinational enterprises. By doing this (and then applying the principle of differentiation) it would be possible to persuade not only capital but labour to take part in this regulation procedure, by taking into account the trade unions of multinational enterprises.

(*b*) The creation of machinery, distinct from the traditional mechanisms, for the acquisition and incorporation of "know how", thus withdrawing this factor from the exclusive control of business.

(*c*) The establishment of the invisible factor of information as an autonomous component in the process of change and therefore as a "power" to be used in confrontation with, or as a supplement to, the present conventional interplay of transformation factors. In this way there would be a denser dialectic of change, on the condition of a more equitable redistribution of the elements of power speculation.

(*d*) Finally, in the actual field of teleological reformulation, inherent in the process, it must be possible to confirm some pretension to control of development above the inertia of the forces at work, including the immanent process of its bureaucratization.

XII. Control of Factors; Control of the Process

In this way, for example, the definition of the social dimensions of change takes direct effect, counter to dominant "trends". It favours above all the breaking down of scales and conditioning factors in which it is possible to face the concentration of these capital sums with the control of the external economies on which they depend.

If this idea is transposed into the social sector, it is possible to see in state control (increasingly evident in education, health and housing) the means of countering (and always advantageously) the *inertia* of capital resources and the congenitally limited activity of business and its perspective of maximization. It is in the control not of factors but of global process, that we can proficiently study the prospect of ultimate control of Latin-American development, and ask whether it is really the public sector in action; or just an attribute of, or the ultimate stage in, the evolution of the super-enterprise.

Basically, therefore, it is in the policies of *urbanization*, *regional development* and control of *internal migration* that we can effectively evaluate the ultimate result of this confrontation. The State will clearly benefit if these possibilities are put into practice (in the ideological perspective of the years ahead in Latin America), for instance in the debates on the "continental common market" on "ecological control".

Translated by V. Green

Michael Novak

Education and Power

IN THE advanced nations of the Western world, there has arisen a new, dominant way of life (and in that sense, religion) among cultural élites. Think for a moment of basic metaphors. "Enlightenment" suggests an almost Persian contrast between darkness and light. "Liberation" is not merely a political symbol but also a symbol for the internal, personal conquest of autonomy. "Authenticity" is a symbol suggesting that behind the masks of public selves is hidden a "true", an "inner", an "honest" self—an elusive spiritual entity, at best. All these materials indicate the presence of a major new world religion. A distinctive sense of reality (myth), a distinctive story to live out, a distinctive set of symbols—and also a distinctive set of rituals and institutions—characterize this new religious force.

By contrast with Christianity and other world religions, we are accustomed to thinking of this new cultural force as irreligious. It is more illuminating to regard its passions, its commitments, its disciplines and its institutions as constitutive of a rival religion.[1]

[1] For the character of the modern "invisible religion", I am indebted to the following works of Peter L. Berger, *The Social Construction of Reality* (New York, 1966), with Thomas Luckmann, *The Sacred Canopy* (New York, 1967) and *The Homeless Mind* (New York, 1973), with Brigitte Berger and Hans Fried Kellner. An attempt to unmask the ideology of universities, science and technology is found in Jürgen Habermas, *Knowledge and Human Interests* (Boston, 1971); *Toward a Rational Society* (Boston, 1970); *Protestbewegung und Hochschulreform* and *Technik und Wissenschaft als "Ideologie"* (Frankfurt am Main, 1968, 1969). For the

The chief institutions of the religion of enlightenment are the universities and, in their train, the schools. The universities and schools have assumed vis-à-vis modern societies the position the European Church used to play vis-à-vis medieval society. They function as: (1) legitimizing institutions for symbols, ideas, practices and ways of life and, in this sense, they have a missionary function; (2) socializing institutions which provide for youth the *rite du passage* into adult circles of success; (3) power-generating and wealth-generating institutions, which constantly disrupt and re-structure the social world. Nations in the early stages of modernization spend great energies on the establishment of schools and universities.

There is a significant tension within the new religion between two concepts—and the forces they represent—viz., enlightenment and modernization. The first is a set of ideals (autonomy, liberty, equality, science, the free market and its liberties). The second is a set of social and economic forces, generating in millions of individual psyches distinctive contours of consciousness—a modern consciousness or sensibility.

Normally, modernization is celebrated both as the fruit of enlightenment and as the further means towards yet greater enlightenment. To be sure, there are not wanting critics of both projects. Some deplore the project of enlightenment, some the project of modernization, while a few deplore both. Some partisans of enlightenment deplore the aims and effects of modernization. But most observers concede both to enlightenment and to modernization a certain inevitability. Critics of either are regarded as quaintly reactionary, naïve, atavistic. "You can't halt progress", people say.

This sense of inevitability is the fundamental religious strength of this new major religion. Many experience this inevitability as though it were the weight of the really real, the driving dynamic

relation of the new class to culture, see *Culture for the Millions?*, Norman Jacobs, editor (Boston, 1959, 1964). For the missionary role of education, see Ivan Illich, *Deschooling Society* (New York, 1970) and Barry N. Schwartz, editor, *Affirmative Education* (New Jersey, 1972). My own books, *A Theology for Radical Politics* (New York, 1969); *The Experience of Nothingness* (New York, 1970); *All the Catholic People* (New York, 1971) and *Ascent of the Mountain, Flight of the Dove* (New York, 1971), provide a background for the present reflections.

of history. One is either in tune with it or else "out of touch".
Those in tune with progress experience a spiritual harmony of
soul with historic process.

The uneasy equilibrium between the tendencies of enlightenment and the tendencies of modernization, however, gives some
grounds for believing that this new major religion is a false religion, that is, that it is not adequately human, not adequately
attuned to historic process and out of tune with man's nature and
his destiny.

Let me describe the situation in what many conceive to be the
most modernized society, that of the United States. Since World
War II, one new college or university has been established every
two weeks—a fantastic multiplication of institutions. Nearly one
out of every two youths between the ages of eighteen and twenty-
two is enrolled in a college or a university.

A whole new industry has come into existence—the knowledge
industry. Besides universities, there are "think tanks", institutes,
consulting firms, research corporations, professional technicians
for every identifiable social or economic or technological or perhaps even emotional need, not to mention the vast army of those
whose labour supplies the gargantuan needs of the mass media.

These institutions—both of enlightenment and of modernization—now embrace perhaps one-third of the electorate. They
have shaped and disciplined the attitudes of a new class: highly
educated, reasonably affluent, enlightened in their social-political
and personal-moral attitudes, mobile and well-informed. These
are the very model of what it means to be modern. They are the
true members of the new true Church.

The very meaning of the word "culture" has been modified
by these new institutions and the sense of reality they generate.
Philosophers and historians used to mean by culture something
like "the best that has been thought or felt", an ability to
appreciate the great artistic, intellectual and institutional achievements of the human race or at least of some part of it (Western
civilization, for example). Anthropologists today tend to mean
by culture something like the distinctive ways of experiencing,
perceiving and acting, elaborated by various groups in human
history.

The first, philosophical, view is frankly normative and élitist.

Each person is tested to see how well he or she measures up to the great achievements of human genius. The second, anthropological, view is descriptive and, as it were, democratic and catholic. Its practitioners are taught to be responsive to *each* human manifestation, however primitive, humble, lowly or merely popular.

But the emergence of the religion of enlightenment and modernization seems to negate both of these views. Against the anthropological view, the modern religion takes a missionary approach: the non-modern should be modernized. Modernization is endowed with moral and religious superiority. Cultures are not equal in moral weight.

Against the classical philosophical view, the modern religion is torn by contrary tendencies. On the one hand, it wishes to bring about an *aggiornamento* of the classical ideals of enlightenment. It sees itself in spiritual continuity with Kant and Comte and Mill and Marx and Freud. It recognizes the need for a development of doctrine to keep pace with ever-changing social realities and needs.

On the other hand, its fundamental orientation towards progress, towards an open and dynamic future (always assumed to be better than the present), forces the modern religion to discount its own past achievements and to regard "the best that has been thought and felt" not as normative but as subject to revision. The cultural standards of the past retain only a weak, uncertain authority.

Thus, neither the culture of recognized genius nor the culture of ordinary people is treated with respect. The new culture of modernization pushes the one and the other aside with the relentlessness of a bulldozer clearing out neighbourhood homes and historic monuments, in order that a motorway may run through.

It seems to be a mistake to think that the major struggle today is between capitalism and socialism. Both are children of the same major new religion, modernization. So to speak, the struggle may be between the modern and the non-modern, between the religion of enlightenment and some combination of other religions, or some new form of religion.

It seems also to be a mistake to believe, as Jacques Ellul seems to believe, that what is wrong with the new religion is technology or, more precisely, the spirit of efficiency. Technology and the need for efficiency we shall forevermore have with us. What is wrong is the vision of man embodied in the symbols of enlightenment. What is wrong is the arrogance of the new class, uncritical of its goals, blind to its own destructiveness, heedless of its own fallibility and human limitations. All of us who have been in part educated into the disciplines of the new religion have been subtly taught that *we* represent the highest evolutionary form of human life, the *avant-garde* in respect to less fortunate members of the human race, teachers rather than those who require to be taught. Besides the old clericalism of the *Ancien Régime*, there is the new clericalism of the university professor, the expert, the modern artist, the social activist.

The new culture generated by the new religion and its institutions is a culture whose fundamental impulse is power—the power to predict and to control. All modern intelligence, precisely as modern, seems to be directed towards the acquisition of power. The new religion is a religion of power. "Knowledge is power", Francis Bacon said, in recording his dreams about the world yet to be created by his *Organon*. Knowledge, science and culture itself are—precisely in their modern aspect—expressions of a radical desire for power, power over nature, over society and over self.

We do not yet have even a visionary dream, let alone an intellectual synthesis, that would place knowledge, science and culture within the service of human survival and human destiny. At present, they are in the service of the naked, undirected will diffused throughout the unguided project of modernization. Or, perhaps worse, they are lost in the confusions of irreconcilable intellectual and social theories and in the confusions of democratic process. We lack institutional devices for making pluralism (whether intellectual or political) creative rather than stultifying.

In universities and public schools (ages 6–18) in the United States, education in values, goals and moral integration is in abysmal disarray. Traditional religions are amazingly tough and durable in the many diverse cultures that compose the American population (Hispanic, Black, Slav, Italian, British, German, Irish, Indian, Jewish, etc.). Nevertheless, our philosophers generally philosophize in utter independence of this cultural variety, as though the social traditions of each imagination, sensibility and intelligence were too unimportant to notice. The "humanities" are not taught in our elementary or secondary schools. For fear of offending the ultimate values of any group the values of *all* groups are, rather astonishingly, ignored. Neutrality regarding values results in emptiness of soul.

The schools and universities are, therefore, designed to separate children from their parents and their neighbourhoods. They snatch children from the folk and subject them to enlightenment. The hope is that the next generation will be more Americanized, more modern and more enlightened than its parents' generation. The very enterprise of modernization entails the forced creation of a generation gap.

On the other hand, those students whose parents were themselves earlier subjected to the disciplines of enlightenment tend to manifest more clearly than others the split between enlightenment and modernization. Already more affluent and of higher social status, already proficient in the ways of the new religion, these young members of the new class enter the limbo of young adulthood.

From the ages of eighteen to thirty, they lack both the securities of childhood and the securities of adulthood. Their enlightened parents have respected their individuality. They have been spared poverty, hunger, disease and ignorance. At the age of eighteen, they spend on the average of twenty dollars a week for their own pleasure. The work force is in no hurry to absorb them and were they to die or to disappear, they would—from an economic or social point of view—count as surplus population. Their instinctive idealism and generosity have been nourished while their sense of limits, hardship and tragedy is underdeveloped. The conflicts and inadequacies of the bureaucratic forms essential to the modern religion deeply scandalize them. Is it any wonder?

One of the essential features of the modern religion is its basic ritual form, bureaucracy. (Even the housewife, Peter Berger notes, puts up a bulletin board near the telephone, rationalizing the family's responsibilities and schedules.) Any thorough attempt to predict and to control requires a thorough rationalization of activity. Even sexual behaviour is minutely controlled by extensive sophistication in physical technique and psychological analysis. Consciousness is altered by the rationalizing experiences of modern bureaucratic structures.

"All power to the imagination!" "Let us return to the life of the senses!" To suppose, as Jürgen Habermas does, that these battle cries of the young acolytes of the religion of modernity signify some new turning-point in the life of the spirit is perhaps to overlook an important fact: the essential asceticism of modernity. Christian critics have frequently complained of the hedonism of the modern spirit. Complaints should first have been registered against the emotional, sensual and neural mortifications daily demanded of and by the modern spirit. How peaceful and even indulgent the quiet, slow pace of a monastery seems to one who lives by a wrist watch, a swiftly gulped lunch, the noise of traffic, the incessant ringing of telephones, the answering of memos, and the stomach-grinding rigours of hurried taxis to the airport. If the modern spirit is partly hedonist, it is also more ascetic than any other known to human history.

We must therefore take with a grain of salt the claim that there is a youth movement of humanistic and creative power. (In part, the claim is true.) Modern secular and liberal culture assumes that, in the freedom of the market place, ordinary people will choose what is moral, humanistic, creative. In turning against modern secular and liberal culture, partisans of the new left are caught in a dilemma. Filled with aversion against choices commonly made by modern secular and liberal societies, they are tempted to choose authoritative controls that would compel people to choose what is moral, humanistic and creative. The dilemma of freedom against order is acute.

But in practice the dilemma is resolved as follows. Mostly, sympathizers with the new left are affluent, well-educated élites. They are the chief beneficiaries of modernization, the privileged ones. But their moral values are out of tune with their social reality. They believe in reason, brotherhood, equality and liberation—but the modern secular and liberal social system is built on power and profound élitism, on prediction and control. Many resolve this contradiction by retaining their power, wealth and status—while making violent efforts to exorcise their feelings of guilt, to rebel for a while against the modern asceticism, and blaming the system's authorities. They are like Christians embarrassed by the actual social realities of the Church.

The modern school and the modern university are vehicles of economic and political power. Perhaps education was once in the service of being, truth, harmony of spirit. Today it functions also —perhaps primarily—to prepare managerial élites for the technical tasks of modernization. Those who accept the disciplines of the school receive for the many ascetic renunciations demanded of them a sort of hundredfold in this life: a significantly higher income, greater mobility, a higher status, more social decision-making power and wider private liberty. To establish a new university in an underdeveloped region is to begin to create a new social class, with new loyalties and interests.

It is important to recognize that the limitations of the religion of modernity afflict those on the political left just as much as those on the political right. Many young American students heroically protested and resisted the war in Vietnam, but it must be noted that it was in their self-interest to refuse to serve in the armed forces. When the laws of military conscription were changed so as to end student deferments, protests escalated. When conscription declined, protests declined. Leaders of the new class first conceived and directed the war in Vietnam and later lost heart and led the protests against it. Sons of working-men enjoyed neither the earlier luxury of saying "no" to an unwanted war, nor the later luxury of scorning what they were unhappily involved in.

Does the political left represent a truly more human way of life, or merely an interest in acquiring power over the instruments of society and culture? There is a tendency among highly educated persons, at least in the United States, to enlist Christianity on the side of the political left, under the rubric of a more moral and more Christian politics. But one must be suspicious of a left composed almost entirely of members of a single social class, and that one of the most powerful and articulate in the whole society. Besides, when the word "moral" is applied to a partisan issue, it begins to lose its transcendent power and to become simply one more instrument of political propaganda.

There is also a tendency to enlist the Church on the side of the right—on the side of capitalism, patriotism, loyalty. Each national state today generates its own civil religion, parallel to but separate from the religions of the churches. It is easy for Christians to confuse the civil religion with Christianity. Both the left and the right are well entrenched in power centres of affluence and status in the United States. They are, it sometimes seems, merely the Ying and Yang of the same religious spirit of modernization—one on the business side, the other on the side of the new professional class.

A specifically *Christian*, even specifically *Catholic*, approach to power, culture, science, knowledge, education and politics may now be what is called for. Such an approach would be a new sort of third force. It would have to meet at least four conditions. Firstly, it must distinguish itself sharply from the religion of enlightenment and modernization, not as in earlier times by way of reaction, but as a fuller and more concrete ideal of Christian humanism. Secondly, it must be rooted in every social class, and in particular in the neighbourhoods and families of ordinary citizens. Thirdly, it must find ways to make pluralism genuinely creative. Finally, it must not shrink from the ambiguities of politics and power, and yet must not reduce Christianity to partnership with a single class, party or interest.

It is obvious that Christian universities and schools are in grave danger of being absorbed in the religion of enlightenment and modernization without being fully conscious of their loss. It may be that as a community we lack both the insight and the wherewithal to offer a compelling alternative. A great creative agenda—staggering in its proportions—lies ahead of us.

PART II
BULLETIN

Josep Barnadas

Christian Faith and the Colonial Situation in Latin America

A SUBJECT with such an immense bibliography, and socially and ideologically so thorny, can hardly be dealt with comprehensively in the space of this bulletin. What I propose to do is to take one aspect of the history of the Church in Latin America and consider it in relation to present-day understanding of the Gospel, faith, the Church and history.[1] The result should be an outline of the problems that different forms of the colonial situation have posed to the Christian conscience, and these can be divided into four stages: (1) opposition to colonialism—sixteenth century; (2) the Jesuit utopia—seventeenth century; (3) the ambiguity of independence—nineteenth century; (4) overcoming the taboo—twentieth century.

I. OPPOSITION TO COLONIALISM

Normally, this is associated with Bartolomé de las Casas and his followers, but today we know that many bishops in the Spanish Indies adopted overtly anti-colonial positions. Now that Church history is seen as both science and theology, the historiography of this subject has taken a decisive step forward and been studied

---

[1] For a general survey of the whole question, I recommend two works by E. Dussel: *América Latina y conciencia cristiana* (Quito, 1970), and *Historia de la iglesia en América Latina* (Barcelona, 1972). I have also made use of T. Ohm, *Wichtige Daten der Missiongeschichte* (Münster, 1961), and of the collection, *50 Yahre Katholische Missionswissenschaft in Münster: 1911–61* (Münster, 1961).

with a depth never achieved by earlier academic historians.[2] The credit for this must go in the first place to the Argentinian Enrique Dussel, who has proved that, during the first century of colonial rule, a large number of the bishops devoted a great part of their energies to defending the violated rights of the Indian population.[3] Not only this, but these bishops regarded their defence of the Indians as an official part of their pastoral charge. Las Casas is not an isolated case, condemned by his own excesses, but one of several dozen prelates and many more ordinary monks and priests who spoke their minds on the subject of what they saw as a violation of natural human rights. Las Casas has been seen as their protagonist because he kept on at the task for more than fifty years, because he became the mouthpiece for many other churchmen in discussions with the monarchy and because many of the extant writings are his—most of which having been published only in the last hundred and fifty years.

Of course, it is also true that not all those who sprang to the defence of the oppressed Indians did so with the same coherence and force, and here again Las Casas is the outstanding figure. Dussel distinguishes between the followers of Las Casas and the "indigenists". The former, with the Dominicans in the van, distinguished themselves by their radical and coherent analysis of the injustices. The latter, mainly Franciscans, concentrated more on particular cases of injustice than on their root causes. These historical investigations have a message for our time. They demonstrate clearly that there is a definite ecclesiastical tradition

[2] This development alone merits close analysis. The theory-practice dialectic is operative and fruitful. Only a study of the Church's past based on the practice of faith can derive an effective message from those who have gone before us. The "perspective" is decisive, even for a straight-forward academic account. Basic works on the subject are: V. D. Carro, *La teología y los teólogos-juristas españoles ante la conquista de América* (Madrid, 1944); J. Höffner, *Christentum und Menchenwürde* (Trier, 1947); L. Hanke, *The Spanish Struggle for Justice in the Conquest of America* (Philadelphia, 1949); M. Giménez Fernández, *B. de Las Casas* (2 vols., Seville, 1953, 1960); M. Bataillon, *Etudes sur B. de las Casas* (Paris, 1966); B. Biermann, *Las Cases und seine Sendung* (Mainz, 1968); R. Menéndez Pidal, *El P. las Casas: su doble personalidad* (Madrid, 1963).

[3] *El episcopado hispanoamericano, institución misionera el defensa del indio, 1504-1620* (9 vols., Cuernavaca, 1969–71); there is a summary in French, *Les evêques hispanoaméricains, défenseurs et évangelisateurs de l'indien* (Wiesbaden, 1970).

of confrontation with the established social and political powers in the name of Christian conscience, and through this to enliven areas of our Church and our personal living of the Gospel that have become atrophied and ideologically blocked by very particular interests. One thing is quite clear—any analysis of the protagonists of the Indians is fraught with lessons for Christian witness today. There is imbalance between the ethical value of the denunciations and their political effectiveness. There is the political ingenousness of many of the bishops, even the best intentioned among them. There is the difficulty of overcoming entrenched paternalistic attitudes. There is also the difficulty of penetrating to the real underlying causes of disorder and injustice. These are only a few examples.

II. THE JESUIT UTOPIA

The Jesuit settlements for converted Indians, the "reductions", are popularly confined to those of Paraguay, but they in fact existed in Chiquitos and Moxos in Bolivia on the same lines, in Maynas in Ecuador, Los Llanos in Venezuela and Colombia, and in California. These settlements have been universally praised by Church historians for their organization and order, their civilizing influence, the artistic treasures they accumulated, the degree of socialization they achieved in their family and working life. Only recently has the anti-colonial, anti-authoritarian and utopian aspect of their character been stressed. Again, the new theological situation of the Church historians has produced a new understanding.[4]

The basis of the settlement system was evolved in the period immediately after the death of Las Casas and the missionary Junta of 1586; the Jesuits reached Peru in 1568 and in the Indian area of Juli, on the shores of Lake Titikaka, carried out experiments that led them to two clear conclusions. Firstly, there could be no effective evangelization within a colonial structure, that is,

[4] The basic bibliography must include: P. Hernández, *Organización social de las doctrinas guaraníes de la Compañía de Jesús* (Barcelona, 1913); M. Mörner, *The Political and Economic Activities of the Jesuits in the La Plata Region* (Stockholm, 1953); G. Furlong, *Misiones y sus pueblos de guaraníes* (Buenos Aires, 1962).

the Spanish commissions, military service, social structures, authority, and so on. Secondly, the Jesuits realized that it was theologically inadmissible to make an acceptance of Christian faith dependent on abandonment of indigenous culture.

These two principles formed the basis for the establishment of the first Guarani settlements by Fr Diego de Torres Bollo at the beginning of the seventeenth century. These were followed by the others I have listed, spread throughout the Indian territories. Their ideological bases gave rise to the defamatory campaigns waged by the colonists of Asunción, the contradictions of the "Guarani war", the mythology of the "Jesuit State", and so on.[5]

Respect for and development of the linguistic forms of the Guarani language played an important part. The aggression typical of areas of contact between colonizers and colonized was avoided. The settlements developed an ethos of their own, without coercion in the direction of adopting Spanish ways, at the cost of being somewhat cut off from the rest of the continent.[6] In the final analysis, "the linguistic policy of the settlements must be seen in the colonial context and in opposition to the colony".[7]

As an overall judgment, Meliá's is valid: "The settlements were an anti-colonial utopia, but never became a true alternative policy to colonialism. Functionally disassociated from the system, they did not dare to attack the roots of the system. This was the drama of the expulsion of the Jesuits, who were forced to obey the system contrary to their ideals of justice for the Indians, which could only be half realized and in the end worked against both Jesuits and Indians at once."[8] Despite their disastrous end, one cannot avoid the impression that the settlement system—together with the Jesuit initiatives at cultural assimilation in Asia—

[5] See the recently published article by B. Meliá, "La utopia imperdonable. La colonia contra la socialización de los guaraníes", in *Acción* 14 (Asunción, 1972), pp. 3–7; *idem, La création d'un langage chrétien dans les réductions des Guaraní au Paraguay* (2 vols., Strasbourg, 1969).

[6] R. Bareiro and H. Clastres, "Aculturación y mestizaje en las misiones jesuíticas del Paraguay", in *Aportes* 14 (Paris, 1969), pp. 7–27; his statements on the aesthetic "Europeanization" that took place in the settlements are debatable, but his general conclusions on the overall cultural clash worthy of note.

[7] B. Meliá, *art. cit.*, p. 6.

[8] *Ibid.*, p. 7.

represent the most lively development in pastoral mission made in the Church between about the year 1000 and the present day.

III. THE AMBIGUITY OF INDEPENDENCE

The question of the attitude taken by the Church to the struggle between Latin-American patriots and Spanish royalists is an extremely complex one. The Church included bishops, priests, friars and laity; Latin America then embraced a large number of different spheres of war. The struggle, moreover, went on for a quarter of a century, with moments of flux and reflux, euphoria and despair, of initiative and disbandment, for both sides. The following remarks therefore have to be seen as generalizations subject to the cautions imposed by the complexity of the question.

On the episcopal level, the most accurate assessment is that there was no unified criterion. There were out-and-out royalists and enthusiastic patriots, and most who accepted the inevitable.[9] There were also those who "adapted" to the course of events. All possible viewpoints were represented. For the rest of the clergy, something similar can be said, although they appeared in general to sympathize with the patriotic cause: this reflects the fact that, while the bishops in each country took a unified stand, the clergy, in all parts, numbered patriotic sympathizers among their members.

The motivations underlying the attitudes adopted are more interesting than the actual sides taken, and merit research. What emerges is the general absence of any serious theological reflection. The royalists made use of the traditional theologico-political compromise whose roots are ultimately in the dubious assertion that possession is nine-tenths of the law. The patriots, on the other hand, had to find some justification for the break, for change, for novelty, and there was no theological justification to hand. The result was that most patriots, like most royalists, based their decisions on political, not theological arguments. This theological vacuum can be seen as the fruit of long inertia, and its consequences have been visible in the attitudes of Latin-American

[9] E. Dussel, *Historia ...*, *op. cit.*, pp. 100–102.

Catholics for many decades, as it is not something that can be overcome all at once.

IV. Overthrowing the Taboo

Traditional Catholic politics in Latin America, which stem from those of the "ecclesiastical metropolitan zone" (Europe), have gone through the three stages of extreme conservatism, "new Christendom" and Christian democracy. All these political stances are based on the presupposition that it is the duty of the episcopal hierarchy to "guide" the decisions of the faithful. Since the transformation that has come about in so many spheres of the Church's life since 1962, a new political Christian conscience has emerged,[10] with the following characteristics:

(1) It affirms the primacy of personal conscience in the whole sphere of morality and aspires to overcome the ingenuous "non-political" stance whose effect was merely to ratify the *status quo*.

(2) It affirms the necessity of including historically based criteria in reaching moral decisions: historical consciousness, signs of the times, sociological, economic and political analysis.

(3) It sees the necessity of analysing past and present conflicts, the endless frustrations, the manipulation of the great themes of Christianity, and so on, from the standpoint of faith and as part of a "history of saving liberation".

(4) It regards the actual practice of believers as the touchstone of any moral decision.

(5) It accepts the militancy of the Third World in the struggle against international injustice, injustice within the Latin-American continent and each country in it.

From this point of view, it can be said that Vatican II (more radical in its influence even than the Medellín Conference of 1968) has led many Latin-American Catholics to a deep evangelical conversion. This conversion embraces sorrow for the role played by the "officialized" sector of the Church since the conquest of the continent,[11] and commitment to place oneself at the service of the peoples who are struggling to shake off the confines of a system that denies them a human way of life. This

[10] Abundant material in Dussel, *Historia* . . . , pp. 149–293.

[11] This traditional role of the Church is stressed in R. Reynaga, *Ideología y raza en América Latina* (La Paz, 1972), pp. 38–44.

commitment has shown itself in innumerable instances over the past ten years, which should not be taken as implying a mass conversion of the bulk of the Catholic population, which has not been the case anywhere. The following are some of the instances where this new consciousness has made itself felt most decisively:

(1) The experience of Cuba since 1959 has led to a re-reading of Christian witness from other Socialist countries (Hromádka, Gollwitzer, Fuchs, Lochman...), comparing of their accounts with the local situation in Cuba (and, until 11 September 1973, in Chile), and regarding them as a utopian promise for the future in other countries.[12]

(2) Latin-American theologians have opted for confining their reflections to the local situation: hence the talk of the need for a "theology of revolution" and a "theology of liberation". This new voice raised in the Church has been loud enough to attract the attention of the rich world, though it can be considered that in some cases the attention paid to it has been no more than to take it as a tranquillizer for uneasy consciences.[13]

(3) Since 1968, clerical or mixed clerical and lay groups have been formed in nearly all the countries of the continent, which symbolize and promote this new Christian consciousness: "Church and Society in Latin America" in Uruguay, Bolivia and Colombia; "Priests for the Third World" in Argentina; "Young Church" in Chile; "National Office of Social Investigation" in Peru; "The Golconda Priests' Group" in Colombia, and others.[14] They all met in Santiago de Chile in 1972 in the First Latin-American Conference of Christians for Socialism.

(4) The most unequivocal example of the new Christian con-

[12] E. Cardenal, *En Cuba* (Buenos Aires, 1972); *idem, La transformación actual en América Latina y en Bolivia* (Oruro, 1970); *Iglesia latino-americana, ¿protesta o profecia?* (Avellaneda, 1969); *Golconda, el libro rojo de los curas rebeldes* (Bogotá, 1969).

[13] The reference is to books such as: R. Alves, *Religión, ¿opio o instrumento de liberación?* (Montevideo, 1970); H. Assmann, *Opresión-liberación: desafío a los cristianos* (Montevideo, 1971); G. Gutiérrez, *Teología de la liberación* (Lima, 1971). Cf. Dussel, *Historia...*, pp. 284-7.

[14] The present level shows the following characteristics: committed action before theory; inter-denominational Christian action and working with non-Christian organizations; free use of Marxist tools of analysis; unmasking of the ideologized confusion between violence as an instrument for oppression to overcome an unjust situation and violence used by the oppressed to overcome the situation.

sciousness in action (though many find it theologically doubtful, and those it aims at find it politically more than doubtful) is the involvement of Christians in guerrilla organizations, the two best known cases of which are the Colombian priest Camilo Torres and the Bolivian layman Néstor Paz. Both died on the battlefield, one shot and the other of starvation.[15]

(5) Perhaps the case of the Chilean Christians who rallied to the support of Socialism (MAPU and MIR) is the best example of a politically mature, non-confessional, yet strongly Christian, evolution. The fact that these Christians cut themselves off from the original form of Christian political involvement (Christian democracy) is entirely typical of the logic underlying present-day developments.

CONCLUSION

The lessons to be drawn from the cases instanced here are far from simple: they can be drawn to the extent that we learn to distinguish what can be imitated from what should not. Their message will be there for those who will listen as long as we do not bury it. According to circumstances—and these are difficult times—it is one of strength for the believer, or of subversion for those who proudly occupy the seats of power, a message that they feel obliged to diminish through ridicule, or patronage or "canonization".

The movements we have discussed show what it is like for some people to be Christian in Latin America. Conditioned as they are by the (themselves strongly conditioned) beginnings of Christianity in the continent, they have had to tread a long, hard road before being able to give a definite, intelligible and effective content to the words of Jesus: "Go and tell John what you have seen and heard: the blind receive their sight, the lame walk, lepers are cleansed, and the deaf hear, the dead are raised up, the poor have good news preached to them. And blessed is he who takes no offence at me" (Lk. 7. 22–3).

[15] On C. Torres, cf. G. Guzman, *El P. Camilo Torres* (Mexico, 1968). Paz left various writings that have been published posthumously in H. Assmann, *Teoponte, una experiencia guerillera* (Oruro, 1971), pp. 163–75; *Diario de guerrilla de "Francisco"* (Barcelona, 1972).

Translated by Paul Burns

PART III
DOCUMENTATION
CONCILIUM

Luciano Martini

Youth and Power

THE exercise of power in all its many aspects has always been inseparable from social conflict. Those without power oppose those who possess it to wrest it from them, to dispute some of the ways in which it is exercised or—more radically—to deny the very legitimacy of such power and to bring about a new social and institutional order in which power will be legitimized, shared out and exercised in a completely new manner.

Among the most advanced industrial societies since the mid-nineteen-fifties, there is no doubt that one of the social groups which has shown itself to be the most forceful in challenging the structures of the powers-that-be has been that of the younger generations, taken as a whole and quite apart from any other subsequent social categories defined as a result of the analysis of various class loyalties and structures.

For such a phenomenon, there has been no lack of explanations. It has, for instance, been attributed to the fact that "in societies with a more advanced economic development, a specifically youthful social dimension has been created in the schools".[1] As this new dimension widens, so does the tendency increase of political groups to manipulate creative potential and consumer potential at the mass level. But even if this is a plausible explanation—schematically speaking—it is important to stress that antagonism between the younger generations and the authority and power in the hands of the older generations has gradually

[1] Francesco Alberoni, *Statu nascenti* (Bologna, 1968), p. 137. See also the same author's *Classi e generazioni* (Bologna, 1970), pp. 127-57.

been manifesting itelf in different ways both in space and time. Even certain types of juvenile delinquency and the deviant behaviour of groups and gangs among the younger generations have been seen as part of a refusal to become integrated into and subordinated to the adult world in order to create their own self-sufficient society, free from the restraint of all other powers.[2]

It was, however, certainly not the behaviour of youthful groups in the nineteen-fifties which spotlighted the problem of the relationship between youth and power in such a sensational and universal manner. In this respect, the "beat generation" and its revolt have played a far more important part. But even before the beat generation "showed itself at a generalized level or at a collective level, it manifested itself on the individual level or at the level of small groups".[3] Even in its many ambiguities, such an experience is rich in significance. The aim of combating the banality and falseness of adult society is explicit. The "beats" are only too well aware that they are immersed in a world characterized by the growing power of technocracy, by ever-increasing social fragmentation and incommunicability, and that they are facing the prospect of life in "the ghetto, the nerve centre of United States society".[4] Instead of resigning themselves—like the adult generations—to the society which engendered them, the "beats" have fought back with weapons ranging from provocation

[2] With regard to these problems, see E. M. M. Eppel, *Adolescents and Morality. A Study of Some Moral Values and Dilemmas of Working Adolescents in the Context of a Changing Climate of Opinion* (London, 1966); P. Laurie, *The Teenage Revolution* (London, 1965); S. N. Eisenstadt, *From Generation to Generation* (London, 1956); J. Ellul, "L'inadaptation des jeunes. Signe d'une société", *Economie et humanisme*, 185 (Jan.-Feb. 1969), pp. 26-34; J. Camp and Christian Chabanes, *Les jeunes d'aujourd'hui* (Paris, 1967); Philippe Robert, *Les bandes d'adolescents* (Paris, 1966). For general problems concerning the young in the nineteen-sixties, see A. Sauvy, *La montée des jeunes* (Paris, 1958); H. Schelsky, *Die Skeptische Generation* (Düsseldorf, 1960); A. Ardigò, "La condizione giovanile nella societa industriale", in *Questioni di sociologia* (Brescia, 1966); P. Delooz, "Le jeunesse occidentale", *La Revue Nouvelle*, 5/6 (May-June 1970), pp. 459-78; M. Livolski, "Giovani, integrazione sociale e mezzi di comunicazione di massa", *Quaderni di Ikon*, 3 (1968). For the situation in Italy, see I. Bertoni and U. A. Grimaldi, *I giovani degli anni sessanta* (Bari, 1960); P. G. Grasso, *I giovani stanno cambiando* (Zürich, 1966).
[3] F. Alberoni, *Classi e generazioni, op. cit.*, p. 131.
[4] M. Maffi, *La cultura underground* (Bari, 1972), p. 5. The appendix contains a detailed bibliography of works relating to the "beat generation".

to negation, from attack to self-destruction. As Norman Mailer wrote in 1959, the only vital response is to accept the limitations of death, to live with death as an immediate peril, to divorce oneself from society, to live without roots, and to embark on a voyage into the unknown through the imperative revolt of one's own being.[5] The aesthetic-psychological-psychedelic revolution, the search after new ways of liberating the individual, "the desperate determination to build one's own world in which violence, oppression, competitiveness and technology no longer exist" are the weapons used by the "beats" in their revolt.[6]

It is not possible here to examine the richness of the beat generation's culture. Instead, it is important to underline some limitations in its style of protest. Its self-awareness springs from the objectives and methods of student protest in the 1960s and the changes which took place within the "underground" movement from 1970 onwards.[7] Its major limitation is that of not having made a more thorough study of the socio-economic structures which have formed contemporary American society. This is the reason for some of the most specific defects of the "idiosyncratic revolt"[8] which seeks for an immediate restoration of community relationships and which attempts to create "alternative social structures to coexist with those of the system"[9]—despite the conviction that American society is beyond all hope of redemption and does not even deserve to be redeemed.[10] According to K. Keniston, the apolitical attitude of the young "hippies" leads to a complete alienation and is the main obstacle which prevents them from being able to undertake long-term activities.[11] It is because of these limitations that although the universalistic message with which the beat generation opposed society was "auth-

[5] As cited in M. Maffi, *op. cit.*, p. 7.

[6] M. Maffi, *op. cit.*, p. 18.

[7] Cf. M. Maffi, *op. cit.*, pp. 40–8, and N. Porro, "Cosa resta oggi della nuova sinistra U.S.A.?", *La critica sociologica*, 22 (1972), pp. 102–17, with ample bibliography.

[8] Cf. F. Alberoni, *Classi e generazioni, op. cit.*, pp. 127–57, devoted to the "idiosyncratic revolt".

[9] M. Maffi, *op. cit.*, p. 38.

[10] K. Keniston, *Giovani all'opposizione*, p. 293. The appendix contains an exhaustive English language bibliography on problems of the young in the 1950s and the 1960s.

[11] *Ibid.*

entic" at the beginning and "fulfilled a historical function by bringing about the decomposition of the existing culture", it now appears to be "historically doomed to defeat or else to be absorbed or manipulated".[12]

Like the "beat" phenomenon, the student movement—with its own distinguishing characteristics—has its origins in the battles waged inside American universities and particularly on the Berkeley campus. But if we are to avoid risky and illusory generalizations, it is important to stress that only a minority of young people took part in the movement of contestation before we go on to analyse the vicissitudes of the student movements. Both the studies made on the eve of the years of contestation and those made in about 1970 when the movement was showing evident signs of recession reveal that the majority of young people are not inclined to become politicized even though they do not recognize themselves as belonging to the system, with the result that they appear easy to manipulate—through the publicity media, for instance.[13]

One fact, however, remains fundamental: the young people who did go down on to the campus to demonstrate were seen to

[12] F. Alberoni, *Classi e generazioni, op. cit.*, p. 132. It seems to me that Alberoni's judgment is equally valid for the European phenomena analogous to those of the American beat generation. For this, see G. Galli's analysis, "La stampa giovanile in Europa come elemento di cultura politica", *IKON* (Oct.–Dec. 1969), pp. 38–103.

[13] For the history of the student movement in Europe, see G. Statera, *Storia di un'utopia* (Rome, 1972). With regard to the political tendencies of young people in France on the eve of the May 1968 revolt, see "Jeunesse d'aujourd'hui", *La documentation française* (1971); G. Fouchard and M. Devranche, *Enquête sur la jeunesse* (Paris, 1968), p. 211. For the situation in Italy, cf. P. G. Grasso, *op. cit.*, pp. 116–18, and the Doxa-Shell survey, No. 9, "Questi, i giovani" (Genoa, 1970). For the situation in Germany, see M. Kaase, "Democratic Attitudes in the Federal Republic of Germany", paper read at the Congress of the "International Political Science Association" (Monaco, Sept. 1970); R. Wildemann, "Les rapports avec la politique" in the Dossier "Diagnostic sur la jeunesse", *Documents*, 5 (Sept.–Oct. 1968), pp. 63–73. For young people and advertising, cf. "La jeunesse ce nouveau marché", *Documents, op. cit.*, pp. 80–90, which reproduce the results of a basic survey of the situation of youth in Germany made by Marplan/Forschungsgesellschaft für Markt und Verbrauch GmbH at the request of the H. K. McCann company of Frankfurt am Main; and *SIPRA 1*, No. 3 (May–June 1968). For a world panorama of relationships between students and politics, see S. M. Lipset, *Studenti e politica* (Bari, 1968).

question the whole theme of power and its legitimacy with a radical approach that was all the more impressive as it was unexpected. During the struggles on the Berkeley campus, the members of the Free Speech Movement were without ideology as H. Draper maintains, and their contestation was marked by an unrestrained explosion of violent indignation rather than the slow simmering of organized rebellion.[14] However, at Berkeley, the images of power which the student movement opposed assumed very clear proportions. Links were seen between the power of the university authorities and economic power. The student struggle implied the use of the first by the second, and the students' condition was therefore seen as that of someone being exploited. P. Goodmann—quoted approvingly in a tract by the Free Speech Movement—said that today in the United States, the students were the most exploited class whereas the negroes, the smallholding farmers and old people were rejects, since there was no need for their labour and they were not wanted. On the other hand, Goodmann insisted, there was a need for what intelligent young people could contribute through their work and as a result they were subjected to the harshest time tables, to acceleration and other methods used in factories.[15] Above all, their refusal was directed against the university with its internal hierarchy, its bureaucracy and its selection procedure based on the triad "courses-votes-unity" of credit.[16] It was then that the students became aware of the sterility and lack of purpose which characterized the activity in which they were employed in the first place.[17]

Starting from the unease inherent in their own condition, the students broadened the scope of their refusal. The result was the struggle for civil rights. But after the Berkeley revolt, the Free Speech Movement differed from the European student movements by rejecting the opinions of those who wanted to see it as the enemy of institutions as such and who attributed to it the aim of waging war against the structures of power in order to give expression to a kind of collective orgasm and bitter resent-

[14] H. Draper, *La rivolta di Berkeley* (Turin, 1965), p. 252.
[15] Cf. H. Draper, *op. cit.*, p. 295.   [16] *Ibid.*, p. 290.
[17] The remark is by M. Savio, one of the leaders of the Free Speech Movement, and is quoted in the introduction to H. Draper, *op. cit.*, p. 43.

ment against them.[18] But despite such self-imposed limitations, G. Serano's observation remains valid when he says that the great merit of the Berkeley revolt was that it "isolated the image of power within the context of an alienation which was imposed but not accepted and which was finally rejected with violence".[19]

That the Berkeley revolt influenced the student revolt in Europe is also demonstrated by the fact that it was Marcuse's first assistant at Berkeley, Rudi Dutschke, who opened up new horizons for the student movement in Germany. But in Germany, France and Italy, the student movements had their roots in specific national situations even though in about 1966 they decisively changed in their character and looked back to previous struggles.

For Germany, B. Rabehl distinguishes two phases in the struggle.[20] One was of an anti-authoritarian character in August 1961, when the Berlin wall was erected, until 1965, and the other in the years which followed was of a socialist nature. According to the same author, in its anti-authoritarian phase the revolt of the young German students and workers was against a life "which appeared senseless, and against the cynical tutelage of obtuse authorities who exercised their power through the state apparatus, the university and scholastic hierarchies and through an active employer class".[21] More than Marx, psychoanalysis was one of the ideological origins of the revolt (moreover psychoanalysis has always been present in the German movement). This led to the global refusal of society's norms and demands. But "since society was seen as an undifferentiated mass, such a mystical attitude towards objective facts necessarily led to isolation and disdain for the manipulated mass".[22]

In about 1965, a more global vision of the problems of power

---

[18] Quoted in H. Draper, *op. cit.*, p. 295.
[19] G. Cesarano, "Il dissenso in U.S.A. e la rivolta di Berkeley", *SIPRA 1*, No. 4 (July–Aug. 1968), p. 49.
[20] In AA.VV., *La ribellione degli studenti* (Milan, 1968), pp. 219–56. In my review of the situation in Europe, I have limited myself to the student movements in Germany, France and Italy because of the homogeneity of their political inspiration and because they are typical of the situation in the advanced industrial countries. For a world panorama, cf. "La révolte des étudiants dans le monde", *Esprit*, 5 (May 1969).
[21] *Ibid.*, p. 223.   [22] *Ibid.*, p. 228.

took shape and the students became notably more politicized. But it was the winter semester of 1966–1967 which brought about a decisive clarification when the preceding corporative limits were made obsolete. The students went down into the streets more frequently and showed their solidarity with the fight for freedom of the Vietnamese people, the freedom fight of the Third World, etc. The clash with power, that is, with the academic authorities and the police of an authoritarian state, was massive. But the dominant problem was still always that of the university which appeared as an authoritarian workshop. According to the leaders of the German student movement, the students were without the slightest power to make decisions within the university structures in which there coexisted "apparently feudal structures on one side and structures borrowed from the norms of bourgeois privilege (formal representation) on the other".[23] The first had the upper hand over the second: the decisions of the representative bodies "lost all value once the rector used his right of veto".[24]

The students reacted against the authoritarian structure of the Freie Universität of Berlin either by forming bodies to represent student power (such as student assemblies) which guaranteed the participation of every student in the movement or by making their own university experiment in November 1967 by founding the *Kritische Universität* (K.U.). What is striking in the writings of the K.U. students is the neutrality of the polemic against the neutrality of science considered as a means for institutionalizing the privilege and power of the scientists. This therefore diminishes the myth according to which the German university is primarily dedicated to the attainment of truth: "truth", as the students of the K.U. wrote in one of their pamphlets—"which should be delegated to the rational individual, freed from any particular interest, is in reality entrusted to one class whose particular interests depend upon social relationships in which there are adults and minors".[25]

Awareness of the manipulatory mechanisms of truth extended outside the university, as in the case of the attack upon Axel Springer and his press monopoly. The demand for Springer to be

[23] *Ibid.*, p. 263.   [24] *Ibid.*   [25] *Ibid.*, p. 212.

expropriated "was a fundamental element in the students' self-defence, and it was an attempt to save part of the population from the effects of the mechanisms of manipulation. . . . The rallying cry of 'expropriate Springer' already showed the extent to which this moral protest had assumed political significance."[26] As the students gave themselves political objectives, they then believed that they could show the proletariat "the necessity to resume the struggle from the point at which it had been abandoned a hundred years previously".[27] For them, the next step to be taken "consisted and consists in changing their forms of organization so that it may be possible for them to assume a precise function in the workers' class struggle".[28]

The methods, the struggles and the ideologies of the French and Italian student movements in 1967–1968 have been similar to those in Germany. In Italy, the abandonment of the methods of corporative struggle used by previous student generations was due to an awareness that the struggle in the classroom does not end in itself since the functions of the classroom do not end there.[29] The university is no longer seen as only a place for the production of values and for the transmission of character-forming notions, but also as a guarantee for the continuity of the ruling class and as a productive investment whose aim is to qualify the labour force. The students of the sociology faculty of the University of Trent—who wrote some of the most stimulating political tracts within the Italian student movement—have used the category of "merchandise" to define the student. The use of this Marxist term has allowed them to define the type of relationship existing between the power structures of the school and the power structures of capitalist society. As the university is a nodal point for the whole system, the first are subordinated to the second or else are compenetrated by them. The university is only "one of the productive establishments of the present social system regarded as a mercantile system".[30] As in every productive establishment, the internal relationships within the university

[26] *Ibid.*, p. 250.   [27] *Ibid.*, p. 252.   [28] *Ibid.*, p. 253.
[29] For a complete bibliography on student struggles in Italy, see C. Vallauri, "Dall'università al paese" and P. Nieri, "Un censimento della contestazioni", in *Mondo operaio*, 12 (Dec. 1972).
[30] In *Documenti della rivolta universitaria* (Bari, 1968), p. 51.

are authoritarian: "the teacher is the lord, the student is his subject ... the means of production produces and the merchandise is produced".[31] The "market value and the functional value" of the latter are guaranteed by the establishment itself by means of "a precise control of quality and quantity".[32] The university as a productive establishment calibrates "the volume of its production in reference to the state of the labour market",[33] and "the practical utilization of everything which has been transformed into merchandise is deferred in time. The merchandise retains qualities which can then only be used in business or bureaucratic organizations of which it does not know ... the purposes."[34]

The student, then, is no longer defined according to his social origin or according to his own idea of himself, but in terms of his destination as a future worker "and in this sense he henceforth belongs to the army of the proletariat".[35] This realization has had the result that, even in Italy, as time goes on, the student movement is losing its specific connotations and its *avant-garde* have joined together in various ways and with various purposes in view to help the proletariat in its struggle.

The alliance between the students and the working class in the battle against capitalist power has also been marked by the events of May 1968 in which the student revolt was the immediate stimulus for a wider movement bringing the whole of the proletariat into the arena.[36] But the ideological components of the student movements were anything but homogeneous, for anarchist and Trotskyite groups played a greater part than any others in the revolt, thus increasing the spontaneous character of the movement. Even more striking was the desire to create a revolution immediately capable of satisfying aspirations and—also and above all—of being a cultural revolution.

---

[31] *Ibid.*, p. 59.   [32] *Ibid.*, p. 54.   [33] *Ibid.*   [34] *Ibid.*, p. 60.
[35] R. Rossanda, *L'anno degli studenti* (Bari, 1968), p. 68. This work by Rossanda is the best synthesis of all the tendencies within the Italian student movement. For the relationships between the student movement, the extra-parliamentary left and the working-class movement in Italy, cf. *Mondo operaio, op. cit.*, all issues.
[36] For the French student movement and May 1968 see, among others, *La Révolte étudiante* (Paris, 1968); *Les temps modernes* (Aug.–Sept. 1968); A. Touraine, *Le mouvement de Mai ou le Communisme utopique* (Paris, 1968); cf. also, *La société post-industrielle* (Paris, 1969).

In this respect, the pamphlet "Nous sommes en marche" is interesting even if it certainly cannot be said to be representative of the whole movement. The document mentions a revolution which "refuses to separate the social from the individual, economy from politics, reality from utopia"; which is "resolutely *unitary* and totalizing"; which has "a beginning but no end" and which, finally, "will be social and cultural because it no longer believes in the privilege of nourishment on culture, of economy upon culture".[37] The dependence from which the revolutionary movement must free itself, covers a very wide range from economic dependence to affective dependence (the most difficult to eliminate).[38] The analysis of various levels of dependence is particularly thorough; but what is even more indicative of the level of awareness among the students of the Sorbonne is the analysis of the genesis of the interpersonal relationship of dependence starting from the modes of appropriation which give rise to property and power. The search for appropriation is "linked to the anguish of inner impotence" but is, none the less, typical of the juvenile period in which one knows "unconsciously or not that one will be productive for a brief period" and therefore we have "the tendency to countersign everything to appropriate everything". By appropriating "things and ideas and even men and machines ... we assure our own survival".[39]

Within the context of these considerations, the search for autonomy is not an abstract vindication of independence but "implies the acceptance of multiple levels of interdependence on a level of equality". Autonomy is won either on the individual level or the institutional level by immediately "taking oneself in hand without delegating one's own powers any more".[40] Disalienation is not attained solely through the re-appropriation of the means of production, but "by allowing everyone to attain every form of awareness".[41] In brief, it is necessary to fight against the monopoly of information and culture "thus instigating the immediate restitution to the group of any knowledge acquired by the individual in a form which is usable by all (the pupil who becomes teacher and vice versa)". By doing this, "education will

[37] In *Documenti della rivolta studentesca francese* (Bari, 1969), p. 192.
[38] *Ibid.*, p. 225.   [39] *Ibid.*, p. 270.   [40] *Ibid.*, p. 222.   [41] *Ibid.*, p. 246.

become a basic instrument of disalienation, thus making it permanently possible to challenge the individual in relation to the group and the group in relation to the individual as much during work time as during free time. As much in 'culture' as in feelings".[42] The French movement of May 1968 represented the highest point of the ideological elaboration of the student movements around the theme of power and, above all, it was the only one capable of bringing it to crisis point in all its dimensions, thereby provoking a crisis of the regime.

The restoration which took place in France after the May events, however, marked the beginning of the decline of the students' movements throughout Europe. In their contestation of power they were not strong enough to overthrow the structures they opposed. Thus, the result on the general level was the maturing of a feeling of frustration, while the *avant-garde* groups became even more extreme in their political positions.[43] All in all, far more important than the results obtained were the social disequilibrium produced and the new utopias which henceforth are no longer the sole patrimony of the young.

Translated by Raymond Rudorff

[42] *Ibid.*
[43] For the results of the student movements, cf. G. Statera, *op. cit.*, pp. 199–239.

Biographical Notes

Josep M. Barnadas was born in 1941 at Alella (Spain). He studied at the universities of Quito and Seville and in the Theological Faculty at Barcelona. He is a licentiate in philosophy and a doctor in history (specializing in America). He teaches Church history in the Institute of Higher Theological Studies at Cochabamba. His thesis *Charcas: orígenes de una sociedad colonial, 1535–1565*, is soon to be published; other publications include *El laicism en el Ecuador: aspectos históricos* (1966); *El sínodo de La Paz de 1738* (1966); *Breu sondeig de la producció teològica catalana* (1971) and *La fe cristiana en una sociedad socialista* (1972).

Claude Gérest, who is a Dominican, was born in February 1921 at Saint-Etienne (France). He studied history at the University of Lyons and theology at the Dominican centre of St Alban-Leysse. He also studied European history at the Centre in Mainz, under Professor Lortz. He teaches in the seminaries of Lyons and Viviers and at the Catholic faculties of Lyons University and is attached to the Ecumenical Centre of St Irénée. He has contributed to *Lumière et Vie*.

Jean Guichard was born at Lyons on 8 October 1931. He teaches Italian at the lycée of Bourgoin-Jallieu (France) and is in charge of courses on Marxism and Christian socialism at the Institute of Social Sciences in the Catholic Faculties of Lyons University. Since the beginning, he has participated in the work of the seminar on "faith and politics", which was initiated by Fr Christian Duquoc at the Faculty of Theology at Lyons. He is a member of the editorial committees of *Lumière et Vie* and *Chronique Sociale de France*. He has written *Le Marxisme, théorie et pratique de la révolution* (1968, 3rd edn., 1972), *Eglises, luttes de classes et stratégies politiques* (Paris, 1972) and articles in various journals, especially *Lumière et Vie*.

Jos Jaspars was born on 16 March 1934 at Maastricht (Holland). He studied psychology at the University of Leiden, the Ohio State University and the University of Illinois. In 1966, he gained his doctorate in social sciences and since 1970 he has taught social psychology at Nijmegen University. He is a member of the editorial board of the Dutch *Tijdschrift voor Psychologie* and the editor-in-chief of the *European Journal of Social Psychology*. He has published a number of works in many spheres of psychology and social psychology.

GEORGES LAVAU was born on 18 June 1918 and teaches at the University Institute of Political Studies in Paris. He is the director of the Centre for the Study of French Political Life and of the *Revue Française de Science Politique*. He teaches political sociology, specializing in political theory and sociology as applied to parties and social movements. He has contributed to various reviews, including *Esprit, Revue Française de Science Politique* and *Revue Française de Sociologie*.

LUCIANO MARTINI was born at Florence (Italy) in 1942. He studied at the University of Florence and graduated there with a thesis on the history of philosophy. Since 1968, he has edited the journal *Testimonianze*, in which his articles, reviews and views about theological and political problems appear from time to time. He has also written essays for other Italian journals.

THOMAS F. McMAHON, c.s.v., born in 1928, teaches the course on the social responsibilities of business corporations in the graduate programme of the School of Business Administration at Loyola University of Chicago, where he is an associate professor. He received a S.T.D. from the University of St Thomas Aquinas "Angelicum" (1962) and a M.B.A. (Master of Business Administration) from the George Washington University (1970). He is a member of the Clercs of St Viator and has also done research in business ethics and the social obligations of business corporations.

CANDIDO ANTONIO MENDES DE ALMEIDA was born at Rio de Janeiro in 1928. For twenty years now, he has been teaching law, economics and political science in Brazilian universities and abroad. He has both founded and animated various research institutes and has published many works both within his own province and on Latin-American problems. At present he is director of the law faculties founded by his father at Rio de Janeiro, adviser to the pontifical commission "Justice and Peace" and secretary general of the national Justice and Peace commission as well as vice-president of the International Federation of Catholic Universities. He was invited to the World Council of Churches and to the Synod of Bishops in 1972.

MICHAEL NOVAK, born in 1933, is a consultant in the humanities for the Rockefeller Foundation. He has taught at Harvard, Stanford and the State University of New York, Old Westbury. Among his published works are *Belief and Unbelief* (1965), *American Philosophy and the Future* (1968), which he edited, *A Theology for Radical Politics* (1969) and *Politics: Realism and Imagination* (1971). His latest book, shortly to be published, is *Choosing Our King*.

BERNARD PLONGERON was born on 5 March 1931 at Meaux (France). He was ordained a priest in 1964. He studied at the Sorbonne and at the Faculty of Theology at Paris. He is a doctor of theology and of history (1973) and teaches at the Institut Catholique at Paris, where he is also in charge of research at the National Centre of Scientific Research and director of programmes at the Centre of Research into the History of Religions. Among his publications are *Conscience religieuse en Révolution—Regards sur l'historiographie religieuse de la Révolution française* (Paris, 1969) and *Théologie et Politique au Siècle des Lumières 1770–1820* (Geneva, 1973).

BERNARD QUELQUEJEU was born on 8 February 1932 at Paris. He studied science at the Ecole Polytechnique from 1953 onwards. Became a Dominican in 1957 and is a licentiate in theology and a doctor of philosophy, teaching anthropology and philosophical ethics at the Saulchoir and at the Institut Catholique at Paris. Among his recent publications are his thesis, *La volonté dans la philosophie de Hegel* (Paris, 1972) and, in collaboration with J.-P. Jossua and P. Jacquemont, *Une foi exposée* (Paris, 1972); also in collaboration, *Cheminements pénitentiels communautaires* (Paris, 1973).

JAMES M. REESE, O.S.F.S., was born in Wilmington, Delaware (U.S.A.), on 27 May 1926 and ordained a priest in 1953. He received the M.A. in Greek at the Catholic University of America and S.T.L. from the University of Fribourg (Switzerland) and the S.S.L. from the Pontifical Biblical Institute. The thesis he wrote as part of his S.T.D. programme at the Catholic University of America was published in the Analect Biblical series in 1970; it is entitled "Hellenistic Influence on the Book of Wisdom and its Consequences". In addition to teaching, continuing education programmes and writing articles, he has served as co-editor of *Current Scripture Notes* and is at present book review editor of the *Catholic Biblical Quarterly*. He recently joined the department of theology of St John's University, Jamaica, New York.

HERMANN JOSEF WALLRAFF was born in 1913 and studied philosophy, theology and economics at the universities of Munich, Bonn and Cologne and in Jesuit schools of philosophy and theology. He is at present teaching social ethics at the Jesuit school of St Georgen in Frankfurt. He has published *Kirche und Wirtschaft* (1959), *Eigentumsbildung* (1965), *Eigentumspolitik, Arbeit und Mitbestimmung* (1968) and *Die Gewerkschaften in der rationalisierten Arbeitswelt von morgen* (1971), as well as numerous contributions to journals, lexicons and collective works.